Queer Families, Common Agendas: Gay People, Lesbians, and Family Values

Queer Families, Common Agendas: Gay People, Lesbians, and Family Values has been co-published simultaneously as *Journal of Gay & Lesbian Social Services,* Volume 10, Number 1 1999.

The *Journal of Gay & Lesbian Social Services* Monographic "Separates"

Below is a list of "separates," which in serials librarianship means a special issue simultaneously published as a special journal issue or double-issue *and* as a "separate" hardbound monograph. (This is a format which we also call a "DocuSerial.")

"Separates" are published because specialized libraries or professionals may wish to purchase a specific thematic issue by itself in a format which can be separately cataloged and shelved, as opposed to purchasing the journal on an on-going basis. Faculty members may also more easily consider a "separate" for classroom adoption.

"Separates" are carefully classified separately with the major book jobbers so that the journal tie-in can be noted on new book order slips to avoid duplicate purchasing.

You may wish to visit Haworth's website at . . .

http://www.haworthpressinc.com

. . . to search our online catalog for complete tables of contents of these separates and related publications.

You may also call 1-800-HAWORTH (outside US/Canada: 607-722-5857), or Fax: 1-800-895-0582 (outside US/Canada: 607-771-0012), or e-mail at:

getinfo@haworthpressinc.com

Queer Families, Common Agendas: Gay People, Lesbians, and Family Values, edited by T. Richard Sullivan, PhD (Vol. 10, No. 1, 1999). *Examines the real life experience of those affected by current laws and policies regarding homosexual families.*

Lady Boys, Tom Boys, Rent Boys: Male and Female Homosexualities in Contemporary Thailand, edited by Peter A. Jackson, PhD, and Gerard Sullivan, PhD (Vol. 9, No. 2/3, 1999). *"Brings to life issues and problems of interpreting sexual and gender identities in contemporary Thailand." (Nerida M. Cook, PhD, Lecturer in Sociology, Department of Sociology and Social Work, University of Tasmania, Australia)*

Working with Gay Men and Lesbians in Private Psychotherapy Practice, edited by Christopher J. Alexander, PhD (Vol. 8, No. 4, 1998). *"Rich with information that will prove especially invaluable to therapists planning to or recently having begun to work with lesbian and gay clients in private practice." (Michael Shernoff, MSW, Private Practice, NYC; Adjunct Faculty, Hunter College Graduate School of Social Work)*

Violence and Social Injustice Against Lesbian, Gay and Bisexual People, edited by Lacey M. Sloan, PhD, and Nora S. Gustavsson, PhD (Vol. 8, No. 3, 1998). *"An important and timely book that exposes the multilevel nature of violence against gay, lesbian, bisexual, and transgender people." (Dorothy Van Soest, DSW, Associate Dean, School of Social Work, University of Texas at Austin)*

The HIV-Negative Gay Man: Developing Strategies for Survival and Emotional Well-Being, edited by Steven Ball, MSW, ACSW (Vol. 8, No. 1, 1998). *"Essential reading for anyone working with HIV-negative gay men." (Walt Odets, PhD, Author, In the Shadow of the Epidemic: Being HIV-Negative in the Age of AIDS; Clinical Psychologist, private practice, Berkeley, California)*

School Experiences of Gay and Lesbian Youth: The Invisible Minority, edited by Mary B. Harris, PhD (Vol. 7, No. 4, 1998). *"Our schools are well served when authors such as these have the courage to highlight problems that schools deny and to advocate for students whom schools make invisible." (Gerald Unks, Professor, School of Education, University of North Carolina at Chapel Hill; Editor, The Gay Teen.) Provides schools with helpful suggestions for becoming places that welcome gay and lesbian students and, therefore, better serve the needs of all students.*

Rural Gays and Lesbians: Building on the Strengths of Communities, edited by James Donald Smith, ACSW, LCSW, and Ronald J. Mancoske, BSCW, DSW (Vol. 7, No. 3, 1998). *"This informative and well-written book fills a major gap in the literature and should be widely read." (James Midgley, PhD, Harry and Riva Specht Professor of Public Social Services and Dean, School of Social Welfare, University of California at Berkeley)*

Gay Widowers: Life After the Death of a Partner, edited by Michael Shernoff, MSW, ACSW (Vol. 7, No. 2, 1997). *"This inspiring book is not only for those who have experienced the tragedy of losing a partner–it's for every gay man who loves another." (Michelangelo Signorile, author, Life Outside)*

Gay and Lesbian Professionals in the Closet: Who's In, Who's Out, and Why, edited by Teresa DeCrescenzo, MSW, LCSW (Vol. 6, No. 4, 1997). *"A gripping example of the way the closet cripples us and those we try to serve." (Virginia Uribe, PhD, Founder, Project 10 Outreach to Gay and Lesbian Youth, Los Angeles Unified School District)*

Two Spirit People: American Indian Lesbian Women and Gay Men, edited by Lester B. Brown, PhD (Vol. 6, No. 2, 1997). *"A must read for educators, social workers, and other providers of social and mental health services." (Wynne DuBray, Professor, Division of Social Work, California State University)*

Social Services for Senior Gay Men and Lesbians, edited by Jean K. Quam, PhD, MSW (Vol. 6, No. 1, 1997). *"Provides a valuable overview of social service issues and practice with elder gay men and lesbians." (Outword)*

Men of Color: A Context for Service to Homosexually Active Men, edited by John F. Longres, PhD (Vol. 5, No. 2/3, 1996). *"An excellent book for the 'helping professions.' " (Feminist Bookstore News)*

Health Care for Lesbians and Gay Men: Confronting Homophobia and Heterosexism, edited by K. Jean Peterson, DSW (Vol. 5, No. 1, 1996). *"Essential reading for those concerned with the quality of health care services." (Etcetera)*

Sexual Identity on the Job: Issues and Services, edited by Alan L. Ellis, PhD, and Ellen D. B. Riggle, PhD (Vol. 4, No. 4, 1996). *"Reveals a critical need for additional research to address the many questions left unanswered or answered unsatisfactorily by existing research." (Sex Roles: A Journal of Research) "A key resource for addressing sexual identity concerns and issues in your workplace." (Outlines)*

Human Services for Gay People: Clinical and Community Practice, edited by Michael Shernoff, MSW, ACSW (Vol. 4, No. 2, 1996). *"This very practical book on clinical and community practice issues belongs on the shelf of every social worker, counselor, or therapist working with lesbians and gay men." (Gary A. Lloyd, PhD, ACSW, BCD, Professor and Coordinator, Institute for Research and Training in HIV/AIDS Counseling, School of Social Work, Tulane University)*

Violence in Gay and Lesbian Domestic Partnerships, edited by Claire M. Renzetti, PhD, and Charles Harvey Miley, PhD (Vol. 4, No. 1, 1996). *"A comprehensive guidebook for service providers and community and church leaders." (Small Press Magazine)*

Gays and Lesbians in Asia and the Pacific: Social and Human Services, edited by Gerard Sullivan, PhD, and Laurence Wai-Teng Leong, PhD (Vol. 3, No. 3, 1995). *"Insights in this book can provide an understanding of these cultures and provide an opportunity to better understand your own." (The Lavender Lamp)*

Lesbians of Color: Social and Human Services, edited by Hilda Hidalgo, PhD, ACSW (Vol. 3, No. 2, 1995). *"An illuminating and helpful guide for readers who wish to increase their understanding of and sensitivity toward lesbians of color and the challenges they face." (Black Caucus of the ALA Newsletter)*

Lesbian Social Services: Research Issues, edited by Carol T. Tully, PhD, MSW (Vol. 3, No. 1, 1995). *"Dr. Tully challenges us to reexamine theoretical conclusions that relate to lesbians. . . A must read." (The Lavender Lamp)*

HIV Disease: Lesbians, Gays and the Social Services, edited by Gary A. Lloyd, PhD, ACSW, and Mary Ann Kuszelewicz, MSW, ACSW (Vol. 2, No. 3/4, 1995). *"A wonderful guide to working with people with AIDS. A terrific meld of political theory and hands-on advice, it is essential, inspiring reading for anyone fighting the pandemic or assisting those living with it." (Small Press)*

Addiction and Recovery in Gay and Lesbian Persons, edited by Robert J. Kus, PhD, RN (Vol. 2, No. 1, 1995). *"Readers are well-guided through the multifaceted, sometimes confusing, and frequently challenging world of the gay or lesbian drug user." (Drug and Alcohol Review)*

Helping Gay and Lesbian Youth: New Policies, New Programs, New Practice, edited by Teresa DeCrescenzo, MSW, LCSW (Vol. 1, No. 3/4, 1994). *"Insightful and up-to-date, this handbook covers several topics relating to gay and lesbian adolescents . . . It is must reading for social workers, educators, guidance counselors, and policymakers." (Journal of Social Work Education)*

Social Services for Gay and Lesbian Couples, edited by Lawrence A. Kurdek, PhD (Vol. 1, No. 2, 1994). *"Many of the unique issues confronted by gay and lesbian couples are addressed here." (Ambush Magazine)*

Queer Families, Common Agendas: Gay People, Lesbians, and Family Values

T. Richard Sullivan, PhD
Editor

Queer Families, Common Agendas: Gay People, Lesbians, and Family Values has been co-published simultaneously as *Journal of Gay & Lesbian Social Services,* Volume 10, Number 1 1999.

Harrington Park Press
an Imprint of
The Haworth Press, Inc.
New York • London • Oxford

Published by

Harrington Park Press, 10 Alice Street, Binghamton, NY 13904-1580

Harrington Park Press is an imprint of The Haworth Press, Inc., 10 Alice Street, Binghamton,
NY 13904-1580 USA.

*Queer Families, Common Agendas: Gay People, Lesbians, and
Family Values* has been co-published simultaneously as *Journal of
Gay & Lesbian Social Services* ™, Volume 10, Number 1 1999.

The development, preparation, and publication of this work has been undertaken with great care.
However, the publisher, employees, editors, and agents of The Haworth Press and all imprints of The
Haworth Press, Inc., including The Haworth Medical Press® and Pharmaceutical Products Press®,
are not responsible for any errors contained herein or for consequences that may ensue from use of
materials or information contained in this work. Opinions expressed by the author(s) are not necessarily those of The Haworth Press, Inc.

Library of Congress Cataloging-in-Publication Data

Queer families, common agendas : gay people, lesbians, and family values / T. Richard Sullivan, editor.
    p. cm.
    "Has been published simultaneously as Journal of gay & lesbian social services, volume 10,
number 1, 1999.".
    Includes bibliographical references and index.
    ISBN 1-56023-129-7 (alk. paper)–ISBN 1-56023-130-0 (alk. paper)
    1. Gay men–United States–Family relationships. 2. Lesbians–United States–Family relation-
ships. 3. Gay fathers–United States. 4. Lesbian mothers–United States. 5. Gay adoption–United States.
I. Sullivan, T. Richard.
HQ76.2.U5 Q44 1999
306.87–dc21
                                                                            99-047900

INDEXING & ABSTRACTING

Contributions to this publication are selectively indexed or abstracted in print, electronic, online, or CD-ROM version(s) of the reference tools and information services listed below. This list is current as of the copyright date of this publication. See the end of this section for additional notes.

- *AIDS Newsletter c/o CAB International/CAB ACCESS*
- *BUBL Information Service, an Internet-based Information Service for the UK higher education community*
- *Cambridge Scientific Abstracts*
- *caredata CD: the social and community care database*
- *CNPIEC Reference Guide: Chinese National Directory of Foreign Periodicals*
- *Contemporary Women's Issues*
- *Criminal Justice Abstracts*
- *Digest of Neurology and Psychiatry*
- *ERIC Clearinghouse on Urban Education (ERIC/CUE)*
- *Family Studies Database (online and CD/ROM)*
- *Family Violence & Sexual Assault Bulletin*
- *Gay & Lesbian Abstracts*
- *GenderWatch*
- *HOMODOK/"Relevant" Bibliographic Database*
- *IBZ International Bibliography of Periodical Literature*
- *Index to Periodical Articles Related to Law*
- *Mental Health Abstracts (online through DIALOG)*
- *Referativnyi Zhurnal (Abstracts Journal of the All-Russian Institute of Scientific and Technical Information)*
- *Social Work Abstracts*
- *Sociological Abstracts (SA)*

(continued)

- *Studies on Women Abstracts*

- *Violence and Abuse Abstracts: A Review of Current Literature on Interpersonal Violence (VAA)*

Special Bibliographic Notes related to special journal issues (separates) and indexing/abstracting:

- indexing/abstracting services in this list will also cover material in any "separate" that is co-published simultaneously with Haworth's special thematic journal issue or DocuSerial. Indexing/abstracting usually covers material at the article/chapter level.
- monographic co-editions are intended for either non-subscribers or libraries which intend to purchase a second copy for their circulating collections.
- monographic co-editions are reported to all jobbers/wholesalers/approval plans. The source journal is listed as the "series" to assist the prevention of duplicate purchasing in the same manner utilized for books-in-series.
- to facilitate user/access services all indexing/abstracting services are encouraged to utilize the co-indexing entry note indicated at the bottom of the first page of each article/chapter/contribution.
- this is intended to assist a library user of any reference tool (whether print, electronic, online, or CD-ROM) to locate the monographic version if the library has purchased this version but not a subscription to the source journal.
- individual articles/chapters in any Haworth publication are also available through the Haworth Document Delivery Service (HDDS).

Queer Families, Common Agendas: Gay People, Lesbians, and Family Values

CONTENTS

ABOUT THE EDITOR

T. Richard Sullivan, PhD, is Associate Professor in the School of Social Work and Family Studies at the University of British Columbia. He teaches courses in family policy, child welfare practice, and social welfare theory. Previous publications have included a study of 1200 adoption reunions, a study of the self-identified needs of youths in permanent state guardianship, and the developmental challenges faced by gay and lesbian adolescents. An ardent advocate for children's rights, Dr. Sullivan has served as a consultant to state and private agencies in Canada, the U.S. and Europe.

Foreword

"All happy families are alike; every unhappy family is unhappy in its own way." Tolstoy's memorable opening lines for *Anna Karenina* italicize an odd and bitter truth for lesbian and gay families. The essence of what lesbian and gay families are still denied is the right to be either like other families in our happiness or unique in our unhappiness. Despite legal gains and a remarkable extralegal determination of gay and lesbian families to live as if free and equal in law and social policy, our families are routinely harassed and troubled by being seen in terms of the category of sexual orientation and not the proper category of *family*. This useful collection of activist social policy scholarship gives a faceted and informed account of the state of the gay and lesbian family and raises all kinds of issues that our families bring into focus for all families.

I've often wondered what the lesbian and gay population would do if, by some magic, national leaders were to approach us and ask what we need and want; of course, this fantasy presumes the reversal of our legal inequality and the prejudice against us. And then what would we answer? One of the terrible burdens of being stigmatized and denied equal citizenship is that the fight against these injustices keeps people from thinking through their positive needs. This collection is a good example of the kinds of forward thinking that will give us answers should that happy day arrive *and,* as several of the authors show, right now in the middle of our fight for equality. If there is one thing to take away from these essays, it is the realization that the needs of the lesbian and gay family cannot wait until the full liberation and civil equality of the lesbian and gay individual. They are mutually reinforc-

---

[Haworth co-indexing entry note]: "Foreword." Dawidoff, Robert. Co-published simultaneously in *Journal of Gay & Lesbian Social Services* (Harrington Park Press, an imprint of The Haworth Press, Inc.) Vol. 10, No. 1, 1999, pp. xvii-xix; and: *Queer Families, Common Agendas: Gay People, Lesbians, and Family Values* (ed: T. Richard Sullivan) Harrington Park Press, an imprint of The Haworth Press, Inc., 1999, pp. xi-xiii. Single or multiple copies of this article are available for a fee from The Haworth Document Delivery Service [1-800-342-9678, 9:00 a.m. - 5:00 p.m. (EST). E-mail address: getinfo@haworthpressinc.com].

ing and powerfully connected phenomena. Gay family formation has been a significant result and continuing impulse of the modern gay rights movement. This collection brings a very useful and informative perspective to this remarkable cultural development.

Of course, historians know–well, they *should* know–that lesbians and gay men have always been at the heart of family life. Nor has this role been restricted to being uncles and aunts and children. We have always formed families and been parents and grandparents. The notion that gay is a category apart from healthy and conventional family life is insupportable. And part of the project this book suggests is that historians tell the stories of gay families better and more often. But there is something unique about the contemporary gay family and that is the insistence on the marriage of family formation with same sex sexual orientation. It is that rare thing, something new under the sun. These informed essays, however, take our gratified awareness of the contemporary *out* gay and lesbian family to a level of serious consideration. The issues raised by this new constellation of family life are not confined to how to establish its legal and social status and protect its internal health. Same sex family formation in some respects runs contrary to the entire system that has arisen to support family formation, gender hierarchy and propagation. Our families are not alone in this. The family itself has changed from the one that was mandated by the traditional needs and then ingrained habits of a developing society. The gay family, however, has no choice but must make its innovative character explicit day by day. Thus the gay family is not only an example of the changes in family; it is a lightning rod for the frequently sensible concern about and too often wildly projected rage against changes in family life. If "family values" is a code word for resentments and bogus standards of family life, perhaps "the value of family" and "the family of values" can stand for the message lesbian and gay family formation carries to our times. Just as homosexuality requires people to acknowledge and cope with sexual variation, so gay family formation will require that all of us understand that family form varies as well. Then, perhaps, we shall transcend with family as well as sexuality the understandable but inaccurate and dangerous attempt to connect judgments about right and wrong with the structure of a family as opposed to its functioning.

The essays in this collection reflect a shared social scientific and policy orientation and are affirmative in relation to this subject. These scholars do not indulge in pros and cons about the gay family. This is not a shared orthodoxy so much as a socially scientific recognition of the objective existence of lesbian and gay families and of the considerable challenges they face and evermore frequently overcome. It is a useful and illuminating guide to the social service context of these families. It also contains a wealth of information on every aspect of the subject and is not only a valuable resource for scholars, but a useful addition to the general interest books on the subject and the personal narratives that have appeared in recent years. This is an example of what social service and policy writing is supposed to do; it can serve as a primer for citizens.

Lesbian and gay family formation is not a minority issue. It is exactly the best way to think through the issues of family in a time when the traditional family is no longer prevalent and the replacement models include some, like the lesbian and gay family, that can do the family's work well. The subjects of each essay here make this point: they concern family law, protection of women-headed households, motherhood, fatherhood, adoption and family ideology and how to make social services responsive to minority families. The lesbian and gay element focuses on what are to anybody who follows the news, watches the soaps, lives in the real world, the very issues that define the social context of the contemporary family. This collection is a commencement and a good one.

After reading these essays, one can begin to think about how to answer my fantasy question of what we want and need. Gays and lesbians have always known–and our family formation but reflects this knowledge–that family life can be a force for good or ill and inevitably affects the individuals within it. This book charts some of the ways in which the sexual minority has taken up the cause of family for the sake of all families and, as always with any lesbian and gay issue, for the sake of all individuals. Editor Richard Sullivan and this group of expert contributors deserve our thanks and most of all the encouragement of a lively attention. The first answer to my question may well be to think of the lesbian and gay "agenda" as what it is and has always been: *the value of family and the family of values.*

Robert Dawidoff
Professor of History
Claremont Graduate University

Preface

As we approach the millennium, policy makers in Canada and the United States are struggling with how inclusive to be in defining the family. Both countries have established the legitimacy of the common law marriage, thereby removing church sanctification as a criterion for recognizing the validity of a union between two people. To date, however, both countries have stopped short of recognizing same sex unions as a form of marriage. There are tremendous variations among state and provincial jurisdictions with respect to the level of protection afforded gay and lesbian citizens. While equality rights and the recognition of parental rights can be safely assumed by gays and lesbians in some jurisdictions, others are not yet certain that prohibitions against hate crimes will be interpreted to protect them. Ironically, the proliferation of hate crimes and attempts to censor school library books depicting sexual minority families coincide with discussions about extending church blessings on homosexual unions in two of the three largest Christian denominations in Canada. Even as Canadian gay rights advocates launch an omnibus lawsuit against the federal government for failure to bring its statutes into compliance with previous court rulings that uphold the rights of same-sex couples, American educators in social work and the social services are reviewing a legal opinion that advises them against a professional accreditation standard that would require their curriculum to address the social service needs of gay and lesbian people.

Differences between the two countries are highlighted in the collection of essays that follows. While Canada has constitutionally enshrined its acceptance of affirmative remedies to historic wrongs in the

---

[Haworth co-indexing entry note]: "Preface." Sullivan, T. Richard. Co-published simultaneously in *Journal of Gay & Lesbian Social Services* (Harrington Park Press, an imprint of The Haworth Press, Inc.) Vol. 10, No. 1, 1999, pp. xxi-xxiv; and: *Queer Families, Common Agendas: Gay People, Lesbians, and Family Values* (ed: T. Richard Sullivan) Harrington Park Press, an imprint of The Haworth Press, Inc., 1999, pp. xv-xviii. Single or multiple copies of this article are available for a fee from The Haworth Document Delivery Service [1-800-342-9678, 9:00 a.m. - 5:00 p.m. (EST). E-mail address: getinfo@haworthpressinc.com].

Canadian Charter of Rights and Freedoms, this approach has been constitutionally challenged in the United States. As Katherine Arnup reveals, neither country has resolved the ambivalence of the polity with respect to full equality for sexual minority families. Promising policy shifts and legal precedents have met with a backlash of resistance to implementation at the level of programs and services that render sexual minority families not only equal but visible. Political mobilization and subsequent legal progress has at times outpaced cultural acceptance at the level of community life.

As Fiona Nelson argues, status can be either ascribed or achieved. Law can confer ascribed status or membership in a category with a legitimate claim on the social good, but motherhood is largely an achieved status and community recognition of that achievement is often the foundation for subsequent role validation. Cultural conservatism is reflected in reluctant validation of convergence in the roles of lesbian and mother. Key institutions of our culture operate to sustain the separation of those roles. Rich qualitative data illustrates the efforts of lesbian mothers to come to terms with the paradox of long-standing institutional invisibility and the struggle to both adapt to and resist conventional role pressures when visibility is claimed and the course of building new roles is uncharted.

Cultural conservatism underlies the response to the equality aspirations of sexual minority families in both the United States and Canada. Both nations continue to struggle with the separation between church and state and with constitutional commitments made before diversity was recognized as a fact of social life. Contemporary compromises by which diversity is embraced and the separation of church and state sustained are fragile constructions. Tracing key legal concepts at play in the strategies advocates have employed to give substance to these constructions, Tricia Antoniuk reveals that reluctance to compromise can exist on either side of the struggle. For their part, lesbians may well ascribe little value to recognition within a legal system designed to perpetuate patriarchy. She reflects on the tensions legal compromise can produce within the lesbian community itself and highlights policy alternatives that shift the focus from family form to family function. This shift restores children to the center of consideration, asks by what arrangements their needs are met, and demands that the significant relationships by which those arrangements are sustained be honoured.

Jerry Bigner affirms the differences gay men may bring to parenting. Rather than drawing on strategies of normalization to counter cultural stereotypes of gay men as deviant, he confronts fathering as an institution in need of change. His review of relevant research indicates that gay men may not be very different from heterosexual fathers in their approaches to parenting or in their outcomes, but where there are differences, they are positive. The greater tolerance of gay men for the incorporation of androgynous behaviors in their relationships and role adaptations may make their homes a breeding ground for the tolerance of diversity that will equip their children for citizenship in the post-modern, multicultural community.

Albert Baques and Richard Sullivan enjoin Jerry Bigner's argument that the greatest threats to the welfare of children in gay and lesbian households derive not from the nature of those households but from the heterosexism that suffuses the community context of their lives. Even where the equal right to adopt children has been affirmed, as in the province of British Columbia, heterosexist hegemony precludes equal recognition of the ascribed spousal status through which access to many social benefits flows. Resistance to assimilation and social convention is put in perspective by children's need for health services and other benefits that accrue to acknowledged spousal status. Institutionalized forms of prejudice may also prevail in the discretionary powers of adjudicating agencies, as revealed in case studies of adoptions initiated in the United States and completed in Canada. Baques and Sullivan's findings support the argument that in the continuing evolution of adoption policy, the benefits associated with lifting the veil of secrecy about a child's origins also apply to the closet door. If social scientists agree that openness in adoption lifts the burden of secrecy and stigma from the developing child, then so too will acknowledging the diversity of routes by which parents come to that role.

While the developmental progress of children in gay and lesbian households is generally unimpeded, that is often a tribute to the efforts of parents in buffering their children from the effects of prejudice. This is true of all minority families, though rarely is external prejudice cited as a rationale for limiting family formation among them. Coping with adversity sometimes comes at a cost. Linda Poverny challenges us to consider whether competent social services to ameliorate the stresses on sexual minority families can be provided within mainstream agencies. She also reminds us that as helping professionals, our ethical commitment is to ensure adequate service even when our own agencies are not immediately equipped to provide it. With a pragmatic recognition of the limited options available to sexual minority families in many communities, she reviews some of the social service needs of these families and the strategies agencies can adopt to address them. The reciprocally supportive network she advocates can serve as a model of community where differences are drawn upon and valued.

While prejudice limps toward the millennium and policy makers continue to debate equality rights, gays and lesbians are forming families irrespective of the ruminations of the recalcitrant. Ultimately the question before us is whether society will disadvantage children on the basis of their family of origin. The question has been settled in law, if not in social fact, for all other minorities. Gay and lesbian parents are not waiting on the resolution of social dissension to get on with the job of raising their children. The intergenerational covenant exists as a social trust to oblige policy makers not to impede them in the process. To that end, it is not too much to demand that policy makers inform themselves beyond elective prejudice and that social service providers prepare for competent practice. I hope this collection of essays will be useful to that purpose.

T. Richard Sullivan, PhD
Associate Professor
School of Social Work
University of British Columbia

Out in This World:
The Social and Legal Context
of Gay and Lesbian Families

Katherine Arnup

SUMMARY. Lesbian and gay parents are profoundly affected by the political and legal climate within which they live and raise their children. This paper explores the changing legal treatment of lesbian and gay families in the United States and Canada during the past two decades. Through an examination of recent American and Canadian child custody, and access and adoption cases in which sexual orientation has been a factor, the author documents homophobic laws and policies facing lesbian and gay families, as well as the important legal and political victories they have achieved. *[Article copies available for a fee from The Haworth Document Delivery Service: 1-800-342-9678. E-mail address: getinfo@ haworthpressinc.com <Website: http://www.haworthpressinc.com>]*

KEYWORDS. Family policy, lesbian, gay parents, custody, access, adoption

---

Katherine Arnup is Associate Professor, School of Canadian Studies, Carleton University.

Portions of this article have appeared in *Lesbian Parenting: Living with Pride and Prejudice*, ed. Katherine Arnup (Charlottetown, P.E.I.: gynergy, 1995); " 'Mothers Just Like Others': Lesbians, Divorce and Child Custody in Canada," *Canadian Journal of Women and the Law 3* (1989); and "Finding Fathers: Artificial Insemination, Lesbians, and the Law," *Canadian Journal of Women and the Law 7*, 1 (1994), 97-115. Research for this essay was supported by a grant from the Social Sciences and Humanities Research Council of Canada.

[Haworth co-indexing entry note]: "Out in This World: The Social and Legal Context of Gay and Lesbian Families." Arnup, Katherine. Co-published simultaneously in *Journal of Gay & Lesbian Social Services* (Harrington Park Press, an imprint of The Haworth Press, Inc.) Vol. 10, No. 1, 1999, pp. 1-25; and: *Queer Families, Common Agendas: Gay People, Lesbians, and Family Values* (ed: T. Richard Sullivan) Harrington Park Press, an imprint of The Haworth Press, Inc., 1999, pp. 1-25. Single or multiple copies of this article are available for a fee from The Haworth Document Delivery Service [1-800-342-9678, 9:00 a.m. - 5:00 p.m. (EST). E-mail address: getinfo@haworthpressinc.com].

On a recent car trip through Virginia, a small roadside sign caught my attention: *"You are leaving Henrico County."* Henrico County: the jurisdiction where Sharon Bottoms lost custody of her child; the jurisdiction where lesbian mothers still risk the automatic loss of their children. I looked over at my 13-year-old daughter, fast asleep in the passenger's seat, and thought once again about the fragility of our lives.

Lesbian and gay parents first came to public attention in the 1970s as lesbian mothers began to fight for custody of their children conceived within heterosexual relationships. Until then, few outside of the "homosexual" community knew of the existence of lesbian and gay parents. In just over two decades, that situation has changed dramatically. Widely cited figures suggest that 10% of women are lesbians and that between 20 and 30% of lesbians are mothers (Herman, 1988:12). In addition, untold numbers of gay men have become parents in heterosexual relationships prior to "coming out," as well as through adoption and fostering and a variety of co-parenting arrangements (Miller, 1979). A recent study estimated that there are "between three and eight million gay and lesbian parents in the United States, raising between six and 14 million children" (Martin, 1993). While no figures are available for Canada, we can assume that, proportionately, the number of lesbian and gay parents is equally high.

Perhaps as a result of the recent media trend of "gay marketing" and "lesbian chic," many people assume that discriminatory treatment of lesbian and gay parents is a relic of the past. In fact, lesbian and gay parents continue to face homophobia in courts, classrooms, and communities across North America. In many jurisdictions, homosexuality is still considered a "crime against nature," and a revelation of homosexual activities can lead to criminal charges and imprisonment (*Bowers* v. *Hardwick*, 1986). Even in jurisdictions where same-sex sexual activities are no longer criminalized, lesbians' and gay men's relationships with each other[1] and with their children remain largely outside of the law. While a limited number of jurisdictions have adopted policies and laws sanctioning lesbian and gay adoptions, many others have affirmed their opposition to *any* form of parental relationship for lesbians and gay men.

A recent custody case in Richmond, Virginia serves as a startling reminder of the fact that the issue of child custody for lesbian and gay parents is far from resolved. In September 1993, Henrico County Juvenile and Domestic Relations Court Judge Buford M. Parsons, Jr. awarded custody of Tyler Doustou to his maternal grandmother, removing the two-year-old child from the care of his biological mother and her lesbian partner. The judge's ruling was based solely on the fact that the child's mother is a lesbian. The decision is particularly significant in light of the overwhelming judicial preference for awarding custody to a natural or legally recognized parent over the claims of third parties.[2] In his judgement, Parsons relied on *Roe* v. *Roe*, a 1985 Virginia Supreme Court case that found homosexual parents to be unfit parents with no custodial rights to their children (*Roe* v. *Roe*, 1985).[3] In that case, the court found that living with a lesbian or gay parent placed "an intolerable burden" on a child. Although Bottoms, the mother in *Roe* v. *Roe*, was successful in her initial appeal of the decision (Wartick, 1993), that ruling was overturned by the Virginia Supreme Court, which determined that the appeals court had not given enough attention to the facts of the case (*Bottoms* v. *Bottoms*, 1995). A bid to appeal that ruling was unsuccessful and Tyler remains in the custody of his grandmother. Sharon Bottom's recent efforts to expand visitation with Tyler were also thwarted, as the judge instead tightened visitation, changing weekly visits to every other weekend, and forbidding Bottom's partner from having any contact with the child (GLPCI Network, 1996).

An equally dramatic decision was reached in a Pensacola, Florida contest between a lesbian mother and her former husband, a convicted murderer. In August, 1995, Judge Joseph Tarbuck granted custody of an 11-year-old girl to her father, John Ward, a man who murdered his first wife, apparently in the midst of a bitter custody dispute. In removing the girl from her mother's home where she had been living since her parents' separation in 1987, Judge Tarbuck declared that it was important to give the girl a chance to live in "a non-lesbian world" (*Ottawa Citizen*, February 3, 1996, A2). Apparently, in the eyes of the court, a murderer was preferable to a "sex deviant." The decision was upheld on appeal.[4]

This article explores the changing legal treatment of lesbian and gay parents in the United States and Canada during the past two decades. Through an examination of recent American and Canadian child custody, access, and adoption cases in which sexual orientation has been a factor, I will document the homophobic laws and policies which still face lesbian and gay families, as well as the important legal and political victories that we have achieved. I will argue that, despite these victories, opposition to our families remains strong, within both formal political parties and the Christian Right. As well, strategic and philosophical divisions within the lesbian and gay movements, witnessed during the 1994 debate over Bill 167 [legislation which would have conferred a range of benefits and responsibilities on same-sex couples] in Ontario, and the debates over the Defense of Marriage Act (1996) in the United States, threaten to undermine the solidarity so essential to our success. As I will argue throughout the paper, lesbians and gay men must work to resolve our differences as we continue to support our families and to mobilize for change.

Although both lesbians and gay men are affected by homophobic laws and policies, gender remains an important factor in determining the impact of family law on our lives. As Susan Boyd and I have argued, "In the realm of reproduction, women and men, regardless of their sexual orientation, are undeniably constituted differently. Indeed, for lesbians and gay men, these differences may be even more significant than for heterosexual men and women" (Arnup and Boyd, 1995). Lesbians can choose to conceive and give birth to children, sometimes with a little help from a friend or a sperm bank. In contrast, gay men cannot father a child without the intimate cooperation of a woman, in either a co-parenting or a surrogacy relationship. These fundamental biological differences mean that issues such as access to donor insemination and other reproductive technologies may be of primary concern to lesbians, while surrogacy, foster parenting, and adoption may be priorities for gay men seeking to become parents. Furthermore, because women tend to be the primary caregivers within heterosexual marriages, custody has been the paramount legal issue for lesbian mothers upon divorce, while access and visitation have been the main areas of contention for gay fathers. As I will argue in this article, these gender-based differences have, on occasion, led to political and legal conflicts between lesbians and gay men.

CUSTODY AND ACCESS

Prior to the 1970s, few lesbian mothers contested custody in court. Fearing public exposure and recognizing that they were almost assured of defeat at the hands of a decidedly homophobic legal system, many women relinquished custody, in exchange for "liberal" access to their children. On occasion, lesbian mothers were able to make private arrangements with former husbands, often concealing their sexual orientation in order to retain custody of the children. Such arrangements are still common today, although the numbers are impossible to determine, given the necessarily private nature of the agreements.

During the 1970s and 80s, with the support of the gay and lesbian movements and of feminist lawyers and friends, lesbians began to contest and, in a limited number of cases, win the custody of their children conceived within heterosexual marriages. In addition, increasing numbers of gay men attempted to secure reasonable access to and, in some instances, custody of their children. In their deliberations in these cases, judges have adopted a range of approaches. As author Robert Beargie (1988) notes: "At one end of the scale is the *per se* category in which a parent's homosexuality creates an unrebuttable presumption that the parent is unfit." Such an approach means that homosexuality in and of itself renders a parent unfit, regardless of any evidence to the contrary.

While in a number of American jurisdictions homosexuality *per se* remains a bar to custody and access, judges in Canada and in many American states have adopted the *nexus* approach; here, the court seeks to determine what effect, if any, the parent's sexual orientation will have on the well-being of the child (Gross, 1986; Arnup, 1989). In a 1980 decision in the Ontario Court of Appeal, Mr. Justice Arnup explained:

> In my view homosexuality, either as a tendency, a proclivity, or a practiced way of life is not in itself alone a ground for refusing custody to the parent with respect to whom such evidence is given. The question is and must always be what effect upon the welfare of the children that aspect of the parent's makeup and lifestyle has. (*Bezaire* v. *Bezaire*, 1980)

In the nexus approach, then, each case must be judged on the basis of its evidence; in order to deny custody or access to a homosexual parent, it must be demonstrated that the parent's sexual orientation will have a negative effect upon the child.

How can we resolve the apparent contradiction between the fact that, in most jurisdictions, homosexuality *per se* is no longer a barrier to custody and access (Rubenstein, 1993) and the fact that many judges continue to deny custody and access to lesbian and gay parents? The answer lies in large measure in the enormous amount of judicial discretion that is afforded to judges in family court matters. Under current family law provisions in Canada and the United States, the paramount standard applied in custody and access disputes is "the best interests of the child." No precise rule or formula exists, however, for determining *which* household or family arrangement operates in the child's best interests. Until recently in Canada, and still in many jurisdictions in the United States and elsewhere, parental fitness represented a key element of the "best interests" criteria. Judges relied on a variety of factors for determining the "fitness" of each parent, including past and present sexual conduct, the grounds for the termination of the marriage, the guilt or innocence of each party, and the "quality" of the home to assist them in determining the best custody arrangements for the children. These tests were used to brand virtually every lesbian and gay man who attempted to gain custody as an "unfit" parent.

With the passage of family law reform legislation in the 1980s, criteria for determining custody were amended and, as a result, parental behavior *in and of itself* could no longer be considered a bar to custody. In Ontario, for example, the *Children's Law Reform Act* (CLRA) specifies that the "best interests of the child" shall be the determining factor. The legislation directs the judge to consider "all the needs and circumstances of the child," including the relationship between the child and those persons claiming custody, the preferences of the child, the current living situation of the child, the plans put forward for the child, the "permanence and stability of the family unit with which it is proposed that the child will live," and the blood or adoptive links between the child and the applicant (CLRA, 1980). The section explicitly states that "the past conduct of a person is not relevant to a determination of an application . . . unless the conduct is relevant to the ability of the person to act as a parent of a child" (CLRA, 1980).

While the revised legislation might appear to improve a lesbian or gay parent's chances for success, there are a number of ways these provisions can be used to rule against their application for custody. First, a judge may refuse to recognize a "homosexual" family as a permanent and stable family unit. Homosexuals are not permitted to marry and therefore cannot meet this standard heterosexual measure of "stability." In a 1981 North Dakota case, for example, the judge noted that a significant factor in denying custody to the mother was the fact that her relationship with her partner "never can be a legal relationship" (*Jacobson* v. *Jacobson*, 1981). The "closeted" nature of many gay and lesbian relationships (*Ewankiw* v. *Ewankiw*, 1981) and the absence of any census category to "capture" same-sex partnerships (Arnup, 1995), also render it virtually impossible to offer statistical evidence of the longevity of same-sex relationships. Given these obstacles, a lesbian or gay parent may well be unable to demonstrate the "permanence and stability" of their "family unit."

Political involvement in the lesbian and gay movements may also be used to find that a lesbian or gay parent is unable to provide a "suitable" home. Coupled with a lack of "discretion" on the part of a lesbian or gay parent, political activity spells the death knell for the custody application of a lesbian or gay parent. *Case* v. *Case,* the first reported[5] Canadian case to deal specifically with the issue of lesbian custody, exemplifies this result. In July 1974, Mr. Justice MacPherson of the Saskatchewan Queen's Bench granted custody of the two children to their father. In considering the significance of the mother's lesbianism, the judge rejected the *per se* approach, noting that "it seems to me that homosexuality on the part of a parent is a factor to be considered along with all the other evidence in the case. It should not be considered a bar in itself to a parent's right to custody" (*Case* v. *Case*, 1974). That statement is contradicted by the judge's discussion of the mother's "lifestyle." Describing the father as a "stable and secure and responsible person," the judge added that, "I hesitate to put adjectives on the personality of the mother but the evidence shows, I think, that her way of life is irregular." In considering her role as Vice President of the local gay club, he added, "I greatly fear that if these children are raised by the mother they will be too much in contact with people of abnormal tastes and proclivities" (*Case* v. *Case*, 1974). Thus, while Mrs. Case's lesbianism was not in itself a bar to custody, her lesbian "lifestyle" was. In similar cases, judges have deemed activities like attending rallies and dances, exposing children to other lesbians and gay men, and discussing political issues openly in the home to be negative factors in considering the application of lesbian mothers for custody of their children (Arnup, 1989).

In marked contrast to the politically active lesbian or gay parent stands the "good" homosexual parent, a person who is "discreet," and appears to the outside world to be a single (read: heterosexual) parent. Discretion on the part of a homosexual parent has repeatedly been cited as the rationale for awarding custody to a lesbian or gay parent. In *K.* v. *K.*, a 1975 Alberta custody dispute, the judge drew a comparison between Mrs. K. and Mrs. Case (the mother in the preceding case):

> The situation before this court is, in my view, different. Mrs. K. is not a missionary about to convert heterosexuals to her present way of life. She does not regard herself as gay in the sense that heterosexuals are "morose" . . . Mrs. K. is a good mother and a warm, loving, concerned parent. (*K.* v. *K.*, 1975)

Having had the opportunity to examine both Mrs. K. and her lover, the judge concluded that "their relationship will be discreet and will not be flaunted to the children or to the community at large." On that basis, Mrs. K. was awarded custody of her child.

Discretion played an important role in a 1991 Saskatchewan case, in which custody of two children was awarded to their aunt, a woman who had been involved in a lesbian relationship for 12 years. In discussing the relationship between the two women the judge noted:

> I found these two women to be rather straightforward. Their relationship does not meet with the approval of all members of society in general. They were neither apologetic nor aggressive about their relationship. They are very discreet. They make no effort to recruit others to their way of living. They make no special effort to associate with others who pursue that lifestyle. In short, D. and H. mind their own business and go their own way in a discreet and dignified way. (*D.M.* v. *M.D.*, 1991)

On occasion, where it has been determined that homosexuality may negatively affect the children, judges have attempted to minimize its effects by preventing the lesbian or gay parent from engaging in an open, same-sex relationship. In a 1980 Ontario case, the trial judge ordered a lesbian mother to live alone. "I am attempting to improve the situation," he explained, "and this includes negativing any open, declared, and avowed lesbian, or homosexual relationship" (*Bezaire* v. *Bezaire*, 1980). When Mrs. B. failed to meet this condition, the original order, granting her custody of her two children, was quickly reversed.

Imposing such conditions is a common practice in cases involving a lesbian or gay parent. The practice is based on the assumption that a parent's homosexuality may negatively affect the child, but that those effects can be overcome if the parent meets certain conditions, such as not cohabiting or sharing a bedroom with a lover, and not showing affection of any kind in front of the child. On occasion, judges have ordered that visitation take place only in the absence of the same-sex partner. Paula Brantner explains the unfairness of these conditions: "Heterosexual parents are not routinely asked to forgo sexual relationships with other adults to obtain custody of their children–lesbian and gay parents are." The impact of these conditions on the lives of lesbian and gay parents is severe. Brantner notes: " . . . gay parents are forced to make impossible and intolerable decisions. Parents who fail to comply with the court's restrictions may lose their children. If they do comply, they may lose their partners or the ability to be openly gay and to maintain contact with other gay persons, which takes its own psychological toll" (Brantner, 1991).

The judicial effort to limit or terminate a lesbian or gay relationship is particularly disturbing in light of the research (albeit limited) which suggests that lesbian mothers' psychological health and well-being is associated with their ability to be open about their sexual orientation "with their employer, ex-husband, children, and friends, and with their degree of feminist activism" (Patterson, 1996). As well, living with a partner was, not surprisingly, correlated with both parental happiness and financial stability, factors which, presumably, would also contribute to the well-being of the children.

The contradiction between the rejection of the *per se* approach and the setting of punitive conditions is evident in dozens of cases involving lesbian and gay parents. As early as 1974, an Australian judge noted that "[t]he days are done when courts will disqualify a woman from the role of parent merely because she has engaged or is engaging in some form of extra-marital sex, be it heterosexual or homosexual." Despite this statement, Judge Bright ordered the mother not to sleep in her lover's bedroom overnight or to let her lover sleep in her bedroom overnight. As well, the children were required to visit a psychiatrist at least once a year (*Campbell* v. *Campbell*, 1974).

A 1989 British Columbia decision provides particularly dramatic evidence of the endurance of these practices. Ian Jeffrey Saunders enjoyed regular access with his child for four years following the dissolution of his marriage until his ex-wife discovered that, in the words of Judge Wetmore, "the father had entered into a complete homosexual relationship with one E. L." Following this discovery, the mother refused to allow any overnight access. In the initial hearing on the case, the judge decided against the father, largely based on the fact that the men were living in a single room apartment. Shortly thereafter the men's relationship ended, and access resumed informally. Eventually, the two men reestablished their relationship, and moved into a two bedroom apartment. On the basis of the improved accommodation, the father applied once again for overnight and holiday access. His claim was rejected by Provincial Court Judge B. K. Davis, who chose to ignore the social worker's conclusion that "the two [men] would be as discreet as heterosexual couples when children are in the home." Saunders' appeal of that judgement was dismissed.

In his judgement dismissing the appeal, Judge Wetmore noted that "Saunders and Leblanc are unwilling to hide their relationship from the child, by LeBlanc being absent during overnight visits." "Surely it cannot be argued that the exposure of a child to unnatural relationships is in the best interests of that child of tender years," the appellate judge opined. Noting that he was charged with the responsibility of assessing "community standards as reflected by the thinking members of society," he concluded:

> I am not convinced, and neither was the Provincial Court Judge, that the exposure of a child of tender years to an unnatural relationship of a parent to any degree, is in the best interests of the development and natural attainment of maturity of that child. That is the issue, not the rights of homosexuals. (*Saunders* v. *Saunders*, 1989)

A 1987 Missouri decision had a strikingly similar result for a lesbian mother appealing the restricted access she had been granted. While the mother had initially been awarded custody of the four children, that order was reversed when the mother's lesbianism was presented in a new trial. The court noted that the town in which the family lived was a "small, conservative community . . . Homosexuality is not openly accepted or widespread. We wish to protect the children from peer pressure, teasing, and possible ostracizing they may encounter as a result of the 'alternative lifestyle' their mother has chosen." Regarding the mother, the judge noted:

> We are not presuming that Wife is an uncaring mother. The environment, however, that she would choose to rear her children in is unhealthy for their growth. She has chosen not to make her sexual preference private but invites acknowledgment and imposes her preference upon her children and her community. The purpose of restricting visitation is to prevent extreme exposure of the situation to the minor children. We are not forbidding Wife from being a homosexual, from having a lesbian relationship, or from attending gay activist or overt homosexual outings. We are restricting her from exposing these elements of her 'alternative lifestyle' to her minor children. (*S.E.G.* v. *R.A.G.*, 1987)

As the cases discussed above suggest, regardless of how "good" lesbian or gay parents may be, they cannot be "good enough" parents unless they are willing to abandon, or, at the very least, hide their same-sex relationship. As *Saunders* v. *Saunders* reveals, lesbian and gay parents must be willing to forego the possibility of a committed sexual relationship, at least while the children are present. Their children must be their first, and indeed their only priority, even if it means the demise of their committed homosexual relationship. As Judge MacKinnon noted in denying custody to a lesbian mother in a 1987 British Columbia case, in resuming cohabitation with her partner "without leave of the court," "she left no doubt as to the priority of her relationship with her companion. It was the paramount consideration. She wanted custody. It was, however, not at the sacrifice of the homosexual relationship" (*Elliott* v. *Elliott*, 1987).

The judicial approaches discussed previously present lesbian and gay parents seeking court-ordered custody with a number of difficult choices. If, for example, a woman presents herself in court as an "avowed lesbian," if she admits to coming out at work or at her children's school, she stands less chance of winning custody of her children, especially if she meets a determined challenge from her ex-husband. Within this legal context, most lesbians "choose" to act as "straight" as possible to win custody of their children. As Nancy Polikoff, mother, writer, lawyer, and long-time activist in the struggle for lesbian custody rights, notes:

> While no formula will guarantee victory in courtroom custody disputes involving lesbian mothers or gay fathers, one thing is clear: the more we appear to be part of the mainstream, with middle class values, middle-of-the-road political beliefs, re-pressed sexuality, and sex-role stereotyped behavior, the more likely we are to keep custody of our children. On the other hand, communal child-rearing arrangements, radical feminist activism, sexual experimentation–these choices are all predictably fatal to any custody action. The courtroom is no place in which to affirm our pride in our lesbian sexuality, or to advocate alternative child-rearing designed to produce strong, independent women. (Polikoff, 1986: 907)

Such strategies tell us far less about the belief systems of lesbian and gay parents than about the attitudes and prejudices of the courts.

It has been argued that gay men face much more judicial resistance to their parental relationships than lesbian mothers. Darryl Wishard (1989) claims that "more courts have granted lesbian mothers the right to custody of their children than have granted custody to homo-sexual fathers." A number of explanations have been offered, includ-ing the supposed judicial preference for maternal custody (Brophy, 1985; Boyd, 1989), assumptions about paedophilia, and fears of AIDS. Such a claim cannot be upheld, however, without much more quantitative evidence. It is arguable that the reason for this discrepan-cy lies in the fact that many gay men choose not to seek custody, either because they are afraid that their custodial bid will be unsuccessful, or, perhaps more commonly, because they, like their heterosexual coun-terparts, do not wish to have primary care and custody of their children (Millbank, 1992).

Regardless of the validity of the claim that gay fathers suffer greater judicial discrimination than lesbian mothers, it is clear that, in the past ten years, the specter of AIDS (Acquired Immune Deficiency Syn-drome) has been a deterrent to gay men's efforts to forge relationships with their children following separation and divorce. This would ap-pear to be the case even when a father is not HIV positive, presumably because of the strong ideological connection between gay men and AIDS and the resulting presumption that gay fathers will inevitably expose their children to the virus. In judicial decisions, HIV-positive fathers have been ordered to refrain from kissing their children and to visit with their children only under supervision. A California court ordered a gay man to be tested for HIV before visitation was determined (Isbell, 1992). While in this respect at least gay fathers face an almost insurmountable burden of proof, I would argue that, despite the vast discrepancy in the rate of HIV infection between lesbians and gay men, the custodial claims of both gay men and lesbians are hampered by the "automatic" connection in the public (and judicial) mind between homosexuality and AIDS, as well as by the alleged (and false) connections between homosexuality and paedophilia (Weston, 1991).

THE LESBIAN "BABY BOOM"

While initially most homosexual parents who came to public attention were women who had conceived and given birth to children within heterosexual partnerships or marriages, in the past fifteen years, increasing numbers of lesbians have chosen to conceive and bear children, either on their own, or within a lesbian relationship. Since the late 1970s, an undetermined number of lesbians have requested artificial insemination services at infertility clinics and sperm banks across North America. Many of these requests were denied once the applicant's sexual orientation was revealed. In some instances women were informed that the clinic had decided not to inseminate *any* single woman, claiming that they feared single mothers would launch child support suits against the medical facility should the insemination be successful or that they would become embroiled in a legal contest should the lesbian couple's relationship subsequently dissolve (Arnup, 1994).

To date, no court decisions have been issued concerning infertility clinics which discriminate against single women or lesbians. In the only documented American case, a woman launched a legal action against Wayne State University when its medical centre rejected her application for artificial insemination. Fearing the repercussions of a protracted legal battle, the clinic abandoned its restrictive policy, granting her application before the case could be heard by the courts (*Smedes* v. *Wayne State University*, 1980). In Canada, a similar complaint was upheld by the British Colombia Council of Human Rights in August 1995. The complaint, alleging discrimination on the basis of sexual orientation and family status, was filed by Sandra Benson and Tracy Potter against Dr. Gerald Korn for his refusal to provide artificial insemination services to them solely on the grounds that they are lesbians. The women initially complained to the British Columbia College of Physicians and Surgeons who denied their claim (*Gazebo Connection*, September 1993). The B. C. Council of Human Rights awarded Benson and Potter $2500 as compensation for emotional injury and $896.44 for expenses. Although applicable only in British Columbia, the decision represents an important precedent in the struggle for the provision of donor insemination services for lesbians.

In light of access barriers to clinical services, it is not surprising that many lesbians prefer to make private insemination arrangements. Here, however, an important issue faced by lesbian mothers is the legal status of the sperm donor. While artificial insemination was initially treated by the courts as the legal equivalent to adultery against the woman's husband, gradually the courts have moved to a position that recognizes the child as the legitimate offspring of the recipient's husband, provided he has consented to the insemination procedure. The husband is thereby legally obligated to support the child. Most legislation now specifies that the parental rights and obligations of the donor are replaced by the paternal rights of the husband.

The issues are considerably more complex in the case of a lesbian or unmarried heterosexual woman and a known donor. To date, no Canadian cases have been reported, but in six of the seven reported American cases, sperm donors seeking paternity rights have had at least some of their claims upheld by the courts. The decisions have ranged from placing the sperm donor's name on the child's birth certificate to granting access rights (Arnup, 1994; Arnup and Boyd, 1995). Such decisions have been made *even* in cases where the insemination was performed by a licensed practitioner, thereby ignoring relevant legislation which extinguished the rights and obligations of donors. In a 1989 case, the Oregon Appeal Court concluded that, despite the statute, the donor had shown himself interested in performing the duties of a father and was therefore entitled to seek paternity rights similar to those of an unwed father.[6] In a similar Colorado case, the Colorado Supreme Court ruled in favor of the donor, crediting his claims of having bought toys, clothing, and books for the child, as well as establishing a trust fund in the child's name, as evidence of his desire to parent (Interest of R. C., 1989).

A lower court ruling in the sixth American case promised to reverse this trend. In an April 1993 proceeding before the Family Court of the

City of New York, a sperm donor (Thomas S.) sought a declaration of paternity over the objections of the child's biological mother (Robin Y.) and her partner, the child's co-mother. The donor, a gay man, had agreed initially that he would have no rights or obligations to the child and that he would recognize the women as the child's co-mothers. Having had no contact with the child for the first three and a half years of her life, he began seeing her only after contact was initiated by the women, in response to requests from their other daughter regarding her biological origins. Five years later the donor decided that he wished to see the child without her co-mothers and to introduce the child to his biological family, both actions that the parties had agreed (prior to the insemination) would not be taken. For reasons he did not specify, he did not feel "comfortable" introducing the child's mothers to his parents. When the women refused to comply with the request, he commenced an action for paternity and visitation.

At the lower court level, the judge denied the donor both paternity and visitation rights. Judge Kaufmann ruled that a declaration of paternity "at this late time in [the child's life] would not be in her best interests." In a stunning recognition of lesbian families, Judge Kaufmann declared that "in her family, there has been no father." Because the donor had agreed to respect that family and had made no effort to "father" the child in her early years, the judge denied his claim. That ruling was overturned on November 17, 1994 on appeal. At the Appellate Division of the Supreme Court of New York, in a 3 to 2 decision, the court ruled that Thomas S. was entitled to an order of filiation. The issue of visitation was remanded for a further hearing (*Thomas S.* v. *Robin Y.*, 1994). When the mothers declared their intention to appeal the decision, Steel declined to oppose the appeal, thereby leaving the result on the books. As Nancy Polikoff (1996) has noted, Steel's withdrawal from the appeal "leaves intact the appeals court decision vesting donors with full rights of parenthood."[7]

In the final American decision, the Oregon Court of Appeal upheld a lower court decision which denied the sperm donor any paternal rights. In that case, the donor had signed an agreement waiving his paternal rights. When a dispute arose over visitation, the parties entered into mediation. After several sessions, they reaffirmed and resigned their original agreement (*Leckie* v. *Voorhies*, 1993). It was on that basis that the appeal court upheld the original decision.

While all of the cases to date have involved only the issues of access and a declaration of paternity, the implications extend far beyond those claims. A declaration of paternity can accord any or all of the following: sole or joint physical or legal custody, visitation, decision-making in such areas as education, religion, and health care, custody in the event of the mother's death, denial of permission to change residence or to adopt, obligation to provide child support, and inclusion of the donor's name as father on the child's birth certificate (NCLR, 1994). As the National Center for Lesbian Rights has noted: "in our system of law there are only two options. Either the donor is merely a donor, with no parental rights or relationship with the child whatsoever, or he is a father, with all of his parental rights intact. There are no gray areas in the law here, and, when in doubt, the courts tend to grant donors full parental rights in cases involving single mothers" (NCLR, 1994). Clearly, these cases have far-reaching implications for the lives of lesbian mothers and their children.

On this issue, perhaps more than on any other, the interests of lesbians and gay men may diverge. While the debate on the rights of sperm donors in Thomas S. did not take place exclusively along gender lines, gender *was* a key factor in the discussion.[8] Supporters of the lesbian mothers argued that Robin and Sandy alone, as the child's mothers and primary caregivers, ought to have the exclusive right to make decisions in their daughters' lives. On the other side, supporters of Thomas S. argued that, as the child's biological father, he should be entitled to legal protection of his parental relationship, regardless of the wishes of her mothers. In a position which has an alarming resonance with the arguments of fathers' rights advocates, Thomas S.'s attorneys maintained that biology, not daily care and control, should be the determining factor in conflicts between lesbian mothers and known donors. Indeed, Thomas' arguments on appeal amounted to a denial of Ry's lesbian family, as he referred to Robin Y. as an "unmarried woman" to whom he had "repeated 'access' " during the period of conception (*Thomas S.* v. *Robin Y.*, 1994). He argued further that public "policy favors the requirement that a child be provided with a father as well as a mother." Such arguments, perhaps even more than the litigation itself, raised considerable alarm within lesbian communities, causing many women to reconsider the merits of anonymous donors.

In a recent article, Fred Bernstein (1996) argues that "involved" sperm donors like Thomas S. should be entitled to legal protection of their relationship with their children. Attempting to steer a middle ground between the positions adopted by both Thomas S. and Robin Y., the author maintains that "relationships between donors and their biological children, when encouraged by the mothers, deserve legal recognition" (p. 52). Rather than extending full paternal rights to the "involved donor," such legal protection would merely preserve the donor-child visitation at the level which existed prior to the commencement of litigation. In the absence of such protection, Bernstein argues, gay men will be barred from one of the few avenues to parental relationships open to them. As well, lesbians, wary of the legal challenges made by known donors, will lose a potentially large pool of donors. While I remain somewhat skeptical of the practicality of Bernstein's solution, I believe that the lesbian and gay movements must begin to address these issues, which, in the absence of discussion, threaten to cause an enormous rift in our already embattled communities. I would argue that sperm donors must be able to "contract away" any legal rights and obligations over their prospective offspring. In the event that the relationships should change following the birth of the child, a new agreement, specifying the newly agreed-upon arrangements, could be drafted. Mechanisms through which these changes can be achieved–e.g., mediation, counseling, or the involvement of some other third party–should be specified in the original donor contract.

In marked contrast to sperm donors, the legal status of non-biological lesbian mothers has for the most part been denied by the courts in both the United States and Canada (Polikoff, 1990-91). Disregarding non-biological mothers' often substantial contributions to child care and financial support, courts have repeatedly *refused* to grant their claims for visitation rights upon dissolution of the lesbian relationship or custody rights upon the death of the biological mother. In a 1991 case involving two children conceived through artificial insemination, the California Court of Appeal refused to grant custodial or visitation rights to the non-biological mother, despite evidence of her substantial involvement in her children's lives. While recognizing that both women had agreed, before conception, that the non-biological mother would act as a parent of the children, the court determined that "expanding the definition of a 'parent' in the manner advocated by appellant could expose other natural parents to litigation brought by child care providers of long-standing, relatives, successive sets of step-parents or other close friends of the family" (*Nancy S.* v. *Michele G.*, 1991). Similar decisions have been made in a number of other American states.

In addition to denying custodial and visitation claims, courts have also resisted attempts to impose financial obligations upon non-biological mothers following dissolution of a lesbian relationship. In the only reported Canadian case dealing with this issue, the judge rejected a lesbian mother's application for support for herself and her children born during the course of her relationship with her former lesbian partner. The court sided with the non-biological mother who had vigorously maintained that she had no legal obligation to support either the biological mother or the children (*Anderson* v. *Luoma*, 1986). Indeed, even the judge appeared to be somewhat taken aback by the stance adopted by Luoma, the non-biological parent, noting that she downplayed "her involvement [with the children] almost to the point of being a disinterested bystander," claiming that her former partner had been on a "frolic of her own when she had the children." Despite his own view that Anderson, Luoma and the children had "worked and played as a 'family-like' unit," however, the judge was unable to stretch the opposite-sex definition of spouse to impose a financial obligation of support on Luoma. Thus, as Karen Andrews (1995) has argued: "*Anderson* v. *Luoma* stands for the unhappy proposition that a lesbian can behave as despicably as any man who evades his parenting and child support obligations and because she is outside the statutes, she can get away with it." In one of the few cases to contradict this trend, a New South Wales Supreme Court Judge ruled in February 1996 that a lesbian must pay her former lover a lump sum of $113,000 for support of the couple's two children. The women had cohabited between 1986 and 1994, and the children were born in 1989 and 1992. The judge ruled that "it is inconceivable for the defendant now to seek to make no contribution whatsoever to the upbringing of these children" (Parent Network, 1996). It is too early to determine whether this decision may reflect a shift in judicial decision-making in this area.

As more lesbian couples choose to become parents, courts will be faced increasingly with the issue of the rights and responsibilities of non-biological lesbian mothers. Many areas of children's (and parents') lives are affected, including medical authorization, visitation, support, and custody upon dissolution of the parental relationship, and guardianship in the event of the death of the biological mother. To date, in an effort to secure legal rights for the non-biological parent, lesbian parents have sought a variety of legal mechanisms including guardianship, joint custody, and second-parent adoption.

Second-parent adoption, the option used by step-parents in heterosexual relationships when they create a new parenting arrangement following the dissolution of the original marriage, allows the "new" parent to assume rights and responsibilities without requiring the original parent of that sex to forfeit his or her parenting status. Such an option has not been widely available to lesbian and gay parents.[9]

In May 1995, lesbian mothers in the province of Ontario won an important legal victory, when Judge Nevins granted second-parent adoptions to four lesbian couples (Re. K., 1995). In a far-reaching decision, Judge Nevins rejected all of the standard arguments used to deny parental rights to homosexuals, concluding that:

> When one reflects on the seemingly limitless parade of neglected, abandoned and abused children who appear before our courts in protection cases daily, all of whom have been in the care of heterosexual parents in a "traditional" family structure, the suggestion that it might not ever be in the best interests of these children to be raised by loving, caring and committed parents, who might happen to be lesbian or gay, is nothing short of ludicrous. (Re. K., 708)

Ontario thus joins the growing list of jurisdictions in which second-parent adoptions can be granted to lesbian and gay couples (Re. C.E.G., No. 1, 1995; Re. C.E.G., No. 2, 1995).

In all other jurisdictions, only one parent of each sex can have legal rights to a child. Thus, the birth mother must relinquish her rights to enable the non-biological mother to adopt the child. In granting a second-parent adoption, a New York State judge recently commented that requiring the biological mother to relinquish her rights "would be an absurd outcome which would nullify the advantage sought by the proposed adoption: the creation of a legal family unit identical to the actual family setup" (GLPCI Network, Summer 1994). An alternative in jurisdictions where second-parent adoption is not available is joint custody, a legal arrangement available to heterosexual parents upon dissolution of their relationship. This option is also being pursued by lesbian parents as a means to gain parental rights for non-biological mothers. Joint custody grants only a temporary status for the co-mother, however, and is still subject to challenges by biological relatives of the child.

While both second-parent adoption and joint custody hold some promise as ways of gaining legal rights for non-biological mothers, the effort to secure them may also pose a danger for lesbian families. As Nancy Polikoff (1990) has noted: "The stress of entering the legal system and potentially submitting the family to evaluation according to standards rooted in homophobia and heterosexism is as much a deterrent as the uncertainty of asserting untested legal theories" (p. 526). Lesbian families pursuing such options must weigh carefully the financial and emotional costs of state intervention against the benefits of the legal recognition of their family constellation, should their application be successful.

The final area which I wish to consider is adoption and foster parenting. For untold years, lesbians and gay men have become parents through these mechanisms. Here, legal measures designed to limit homosexuals' access to children have forced prospective adoptive or foster parents to present themselves to social service agencies as single individuals, regardless of their relationship status. The question of adoption reveals in a dramatic fashion the fact that many segments of society still harbor irrational and unfounded fears and prejudices about the dangers posed by relationships between lesbians or gay men and children. Those fears persist despite the almost complete lack of evidence of child abuse perpetrated by lesbians or gay men. Thus, lesbians and gay men wishing to adopt or foster children still face enormous barriers. For example, with the exception of British Columbia, lesbians and gay men in Canada cannot adopt a child as a couple. Instead, one of the members of a couple must apply for adoption. If that application is successful, then the partner may, in some jurisdictions, apply for a second-parent adoption.

Adoption can follow several routes including public adoption through a publicly mandated or chartered agency such as the Children's Aid Society, private adoption through an independent agency, independent adoption assisted through the court by privately hired lawyers, and international adoption, usually arranged privately and shepherded through the immigration and family court systems with fairly minimal state oversight. With the exception of public adoption, all of these forms are costly, and any type of adoption is fraught with uncertainty and long periods of waiting. For lesbians and gay men wishing to adopt, however, these problems are compounded by legal barriers. In only two states in the United States, New York and California, are lesbians and gays legally protected against discrimination in the adoption process. Even that protection does not mean, of course, that individuals will not face discrimination; it offers some limited guarantee that an individual will not be turned down solely on the basis of sexual orientation. In two other states, Florida and New Hampshire, openly lesbian and gay prospective parents are prohibited by law from adoption. In Ohio, the Supreme Court interpreted the state adoption law in such a way as to allow a gay man to adopt. In all other states, no specific legislation related to sexual orientation and adoption exists (Miller, 1993). It must be noted, however, that in 38 American states, the Department of Social Services is administered by the county, as opposed to state regulated. That means that there can be huge variations across the state on how decisions on adoption and fostering for same-sex couples are determined.

For gay men, for whom fewer avenues to parenting are available, these barriers may be especially punishing. Yet, ironically, during the 1994 debate in Ontario over Bill 167 [legislation designed to extend a range of rights and obligations to same-sex partners and their offspring], it was primarily gay men who were prepared to urge the New Democratic Party government to abandon the adoption issue, arguing that its "controversial" nature threatened to jeopardize the entire bill. That move, and its aftermath, highlighted once again the need for ongoing political discussion of the complex issues that face our families.

CONCLUSION

The legal position of lesbian and gay parents has improved considerably since the first lesbian custody cases began to appear before the courts in Canada, the United States and elsewhere, some twenty years ago. Lesbian and gay families are gaining visibility and acceptance in schools, day care centers, and communities across North America. Lesbians and gay men are contesting homophobic laws and practices in the areas of adoption, foster parenting, and child custody. The passage on May 8, 1996 of Bill C-33, legislation which amended the Canadian Human Rights Act to include sexual orientation as a prohibited ground for discrimination, is the latest in a series of important victories. Today, it is no longer a certainty in most jurisdictions that lesbian or gay parents will lose custody of their children. Despite these gains, however, lesbian and gay parents still risk losing their children and many are fighting these battles every day. As activists, as advocates, as parents and as friends, we must work together to support their struggles, and to fight for legal recognition of our families. Recognition in the courts will give legal foundation to the legitimacy of claims-making on behalf of the equality rights of our children. Further recognition of their equality rights can move us closer to the assurance of equality of access and treatment in the other arenas of social policy that have a direct effect on families.

NOTES

1. The Defense of Marriage Act (DOMA), passed by Congress and signed by President Clinton in September 1996, defines marriage as "a legal union between one man and one woman as husband and wife." Under this legislation, same-sex unions could not be marriages.

2. Grandparents fall within the category of third parties. It is worth noting that Tyler's biological father supported Sharon Bottoms' bid for custody.

3. The Virginia Supreme Court found that living conditions would "impose an intolerable burden upon her [the child] by reason of the social condemnation attached to them." The court noted as well that "the father's unfitness is manifested by his willingness to impose this burden upon [his daughter] in exchange for his own gratification." 694.

4. Mary Ward subsequently died of a heart attack on January 21, 1997 at the age of 47.

5. Not all cases which appear before the courts are reported in legal journals. It is a common practice in cases in which homosexuality or lesbianism is a factor to seal the records, ostensibly to protect the privacy of the individuals involved. This practice presents a problem for both lawyers and researchers in the field of lesbian custody. Those cases which are reported become accessible to judges and lawyers for their use in future cases, and thereby assume an importance beyond their individual significance.

6. In *Kevin N. McIntyre v. Linden Crouch,* while the insemination was not performed by a licensed practitioner, the court determined that the relevant Oregon legislation regarding donor insemination did apply. That legislation specified that, when an insemination is performed by a licensed practitioner, the donor has "no right, obligation or interest with respect to a child born as a result of artificial insemination" and the child has "no right, obligation or interest with respect" to the donor. ORS 109.239 section 5, 1 and 2. *McIntyre v. Crouch,* 780 P. 2d 239 (Or. App. 1989). Despite that finding, the court ruled that, if the donor could demonstrate that an agreement had existed between himself and the mother regarding his parental involvement

with the child, then his constitutional rights would have been violated. They directed him to a lower court to make arguments on this issue.

7. Thomas Steel died of complications from AIDS on July 18, 1998.

8. Indeed, the majority in the appellate court decision defined the case explicitly in gender terms. "The notion that a lesbian mother should enjoy a parental relationship with her daughter but a gay man should not is so innately discriminatory as to be unworthy of comment." *Thomas S.* v. *Robin Y.*, 618 N.Y.S.2d 360 (App. Div. 1994).

9. According to a 1996 newsletter of the Gay and Lesbian Parents Coalition International (GLPCI), the following jurisdictions have granted at least one second-parent adoption: Alaska, California, Colorado, District of Columbia, Illinois, Indiana, Iowa, Massachusetts, Michigan, Minnesota, Nevada, New Jersey, New York, Ohio, Oregon, Pennsylvania, Rhode Island, Texas, Vermont, and Washington. England also recently granted a second-parent adoption. GLPCI Network, Winter/Spring 1996 Issue, 14. On November 4, 1996, full adoption rights were extended to same-sex couples in British Columbia. The Parent's Network, 2, 2 (June/July 1996).

REFERENCES

Andrews, K. (1995). Ancient affections: Gays, lesbians and family status. In K. Arnup (Ed.), *Lesbian parenting: Living with pride and prejudice* (pp. 367-382). Charlottetown: Gynergy.

Arnup, K. (1994). Finding fathers: Artificial insemination, lesbians, and the law. *Canadian Journal of Women and the Law 7(1)*, 97-115.

Arnup, K. & Boyd, S. (1995). Familial disputes? Sperm donors, lesbian mothers, and legal parenthood. In D. Herman & C. Stychin (Eds.), *Legal inversions: Lesbians, gay men, and the politics of law* (pp. 79-102). Philadelphia: Temple University Press.

Arnup, K. (1989). Mothers just like others: Lesbians, divorce, and child custody in Canada. *Canadian Journal of Women and the Law, 3*, 18-32.

Arnup, K. (1995). Still hidden in the household. Paper presented at the Annual Meeting of the Canadian Lesbian and Gay Studies Association, Montreal, PQ.

Bateman, M. (1992). Lesbians, gays and child custody: An Australian legal history. *Australian Gay and Lesbian Law Journal, 1*, 49-62.

Beargie, R. A. (1988). Custody determinations involving the homosexual parent. *Family Law Quarterly, 22 (1)*, 71-86.

Bernstein, F. A. (1996). This child does have two mothers . . . and a sperm donor with visitation. *Review of Law and Social Change, 22 (1)*, 1-58.

Bezaire v. *Bezaire*, 20 R.F.L. (2d) 365 (Ont. C.A. 1980).

Bottoms v. *Bottoms*, 457 S.E. 2d 102 (Va. 1995).

Bowers v. *Hardwick*, 106 S.Ct. 2841 (1986).

Boyd, S. (1989). From gender specificity to gender neutrality? Ideologies in Canadian child custody law. In C. Smart & S. Sevenhuijsen (Eds.), *Child care and the politics of gender* (pp. 126-157). London: Routledge.

Brantner, P. A. (1991). When mommy or daddy is gay: Developing constitutional standards for custody decisions. *Hastings Women's Law Journal, 3 (1)*, 105-107.

Brophy, J. (1985). Child care and the growth of power: The status of mothers in child custody disputes. In C. Smart & J. Brophy (Eds.), *Women in Law* (pp. 97-116). London: Routledge.

Case v. *Case*, 18 R.F.L. 138 (Sask. Queen's Bench, 1974).

Children's Law Reform Act, R.S.O., c. 68, section 24 (1980).

D.M. v. *M.D.* 94 Sask. R. 315; S.J. No. 672 (1991).

Elliott v. *Elliott*, B.C.J. No. 43 (BCSC), 22 (1987).

Ewankiw v. *Ewankiw*, M.J. No. 692 (Man. Q.B., Family Division, 1994).

GLPCI Network (1996 Fall), p. 3.

Gross, W. (1986). Judging the best interests of the child: Child custody and the homosexual parent. *Canadian Journal of Women and the Law, 1*, 505-531.

Herman, E. (1988). The romance of lesbian motherhood. *Sojourner: The Women's Forum*, March.

Interest of R.C. 775 P2d 27 (Colo. 1989).

Isbell, M. T. (1992). *HIV and family law: A survey.* Toronto: Lambda Legal Defense and Education Fund.

Jacobson v. *Jacobson*, 314 N.W. 2d 78 (N.D. 1981).

K. v. *K.*, 23 R.F.L. 63 (Alta. Prov. Ct, 1975).

Leckie v. *Voorhies*, Case No. 60-92-06326 (Ore. Circuit Court, April 5, 1993), (unreported); and *Leckie* v. *Voorhies*, No. A79785, May 25, 1994, 128 Ore. App. 289.

Lesbian couple charge doctor and college with discrimination (September 1993), *Gazebo Connection, 14 (8)*, 2.

Martin, A. (1993). *The lesbian and gay parenting handbook.* New York: Harper Collins.

McGuire, M. & Alexander, N. (1985). Artificial insemination of single women. *Fertility and Sterility, 43*, 182-184.

Millbank, J. (1992). Lesbian mothers, gay fathers: Sameness and difference. *Australian Gay and Lesbian Law Journal, 2*, 21-40.

Miller, B. (1979). Gay fathers and their children. *The Family Coordinator, 28*, 544-52.

National Center for Lesbian Rights (1993). Lesbians choosing motherhood: Legal implications of donor insemination and co-parenting. Reprinted in William B. Rubenstein (Ed.), *Lesbians, gay men, and the law.* New York: New Press, 543.

Ottawa Citizen, February 3, 1996, A2.

Patterson, C. J. (1996). Lesbian and gay parents and their children. In R. C. Savin-Williams & K. M. Cohen (Eds.), *The lives of lesbians, gays, and bisexuals: Adults to children* (pp. 281-298). Orlando, FL: Harcourt Brace.

Polikoff, N. (1986). Lesbian mothers, lesbian families: Legal obstacles, legal challenges. *Review of Law and Social Change, 14*, 907-916.

Polikoff, N. D. (1990-91). This child does have two mothers: Redefining parenthood to meet the needs of children in lesbian-mother and other nontraditional families. *Georgetown Law Journal, 78*, 459-575.

Polikoff, N. (1996). What's biology got to do with it? Cited in Fred A. Bernstein, This child does have two mothers . . . and a sperm donor with visitation. *Review of Law and Social Change, 22 (1)*, note 218, p. 37.

Rubenstein, W. B. (Ed.) (1993). *Lesbians, gay men, and the law.* New York: New Press.

Saunders v. *Saunders* (1989), 20 R.F.L. (3d) 368 (B.C. Co. Ct.).

S.E.G. v. *R.A.G.* 735 S.W. 2d 164 (Mo. Ct. App. 1987); cited in William Rubenstein, (Ed.) (1993). *Lesbians, gay men, and the law* (pp. 496-497). New York: New Press.

Smedes v. *Wayne State University*, No. 80-725-83 (E.D. Mich., filed July 15, 1980).

Thomas S. v. *Robin Y.* 1994 N.Y. App. Div., Lexis 11385.

Wartik, N. (1993, November/December). Virginia is no place for lesbian mothers. *Ms.*, 89.

Weston, K. (1991). Parenting in the age of AIDS. In *Families we choose: Lesbians, gays, kinship.* New York: Columbia University Press.

Wishard, D. R. (1989). Out of the closets and into the courts: Homosexual fathers and child custody. *Dickinson Law Review, 93*, 420.

Lesbian Families:
Achieving Motherhood

Fiona Nelson

SUMMARY. For lesbian women, achieving the status of "mother" is often a complicated and conflict-ridden process. There can be great disagreement among the social bodies who are empowered to validate women as mothers (and domestic groups as families), including family members themselves, as to who is or is not a mother. These notions, often based on heterosexual, heterosexist and patriarchal conceptualizations of "the family" create family experiences and family dynamics that are unique to lesbian women. Furthermore, different types of lesbian families, for example blended families and those created by donor insemination, share some experiences related to their social context, but also differ in terms of their family dynamics. Social and community services and programs directed toward families need to recognize the existence of lesbian families, the variety of forms of lesbian families, and the specialized needs of different types of lesbian families. *[Article copies available for a fee from The Haworth Document Delivery Service: 1-800-342-9678. E-mail address: getinfo@haworthpressinc.com <Website: http://www.haworthpressinc.com>]*

KEYWORDS. Lesbian motherhood, parenting adjustment, achieved and ascribed status, social services

---

Fiona Nelson is affiliated with the Department of Sociology, University of Alberta.

From the author's *Lesbian Motherhood: An Exploration of Canadian Lesbian Families*, chapters 3-5, ©University of Toronto Press Inc., 1996 (adapted with permission).

A partial draft of this paper was presented at the Canadian Sociology and Anthropology Association annual meeting in St. Catharines, June 1996.

[Haworth co-indexing entry note]: "Lesbian Families: Achieving Motherhood." Nelson, Fiona. Co-published simultaneously in *Journal of Gay & Lesbian Social Services* (Harrington Park Press, an imprint of The Haworth Press, Inc.) Vol. 10, No. 1, 1999, pp. 27-46; and: *Queer Families, Common Agendas: Gay People, Lesbians, and Family Values* (ed: T. Richard Sullivan) Harrington Park Press, an imprint of The Haworth Press, Inc., 1999, pp. 27-46. Single or multiple copies of this article are available for a fee from The Haworth Document Delivery Service [1-800-342-9678, 9:00 a.m. - 5:00 p.m. (EST). E-mail address: getinfo@haworthpressinc.com].

ACHIEVING MOTHERHOOD

This paper will discuss motherhood as an achieved status and consider how this notion relates to lesbian mothers. In Sociology, an "achieved status" is a social position one acquires through one's activities whereas an "ascribed status" is a position one occupies by virtue of particular characteristics. So, for example, sociologists would see "aboriginal" as an ascribed status and "student," "CEO," or "mother" as achieved statuses. By this definition of achieved status, we can see that the role one plays, and the activities performed in that role, are closely linked to, and constitutive of, a particular achieved status. An achieved status cannot always, however, simply be reduced to role and tasks. For example, ideally, anyone could play the role and perform the tasks associated with the achieved status of "student," and be acknowledged as such. But motherhood is not so simple. Although almost any adult could play the role and perform many of the tasks associated with mothering (apart from gestation, birthing and breastfeeding), not everyone who does so achieves the status of "mother." And this underscores a very important, although usually overlooked, component of achieved status. For a status to be achieved, there must be some recognition and acknowledgement from a "valid" body or bodies, individual or institutional, that the status has been achieved. And this recognition and acknowledgement does not rest solely on the roles played or tasks completed. When it comes to gaining this recognition and acknowledgement, lesbian mothers, as mothers, are severely disadvantaged. In fact, many of the issues and challenges faced by lesbian mothers can be traced to general social reluctance to acknowledge lesbian mothers as mothers and lesbian families as families.

There are different individuals and institutions who can validly recognize different achieved statuses, although generally for any given achieved status the acknowledgement of some institutions or persons will carry more weight than that of others. For example, the acknowledgment of your family and friends that you are a "minister of God" can hold little weight if no church recognizes you as such. By the same token, different individuals or institutions might assess the same behavior very differently. For example, the behavior that makes you a "civil rights activist" in your community might make you a "subversive" in the eyes of the state. Furthermore, different levels of acknowledgement can inform each other. For example, religious doctrines and state legislation can inform each other and either of these can both reflect and inform the terms by which the population understands their lives.

"Mother," I would suggest, is an extremely complex and highly contested achieved status. The individuals and institutions who are empowered to recognize and acknowledge some people as mothers exist at numerous social levels and in a myriad of social contexts. Each carries a different weight of authority and they certainly, at times, disagree with each other. We can conceptualize these individuals and institutions as a web within which lesbian families exist and within which they struggle both to identify themselves and to achieve recognition and acknowledgement from others.

For the purposes of this discussion I will claim that there are at least seven distinct, though broadly defined, "bodies" that are empowered to recognize and validate the achieved status of "mother." The first of these is the state which has, provincial variations notwithstanding, been rather reluctant to extend legislative recognition and protection to lesbian families in general, and lesbian mothers in particular. Next is "the church" which plays a vital role for many people in identifying what an appropriate family form is and who appropriate family members are. Third is the medical industry, the practitioners of which wield a great deal of power when it comes to deciding who will be acknowledged as a mother, the valid means of becoming a mother, and even who "deserves" to become a mother. I would contend that these three groups form the fundamental ballast of what has been called a "motherhood hierarchy" (DiLapi, 1989). DiLapi argues that this "motherhood hierarchy operates through formal and informal social policy. Ultimately it determines who has access to reproductive health care and parenthood. Those who fit the 'appropriate mother' stereotype have the greatest access to information and resources to parent." A fourth body empowered to recognize and validate the status of "mother" is that nebulous entity, society at large. For present purposes, "society at large" can be broken down into at least three distinct subgroups: the friends surrounding the lesbian family, the lesbian and/or gay community, and the heterosexual community. Fifth is a group I am separating from "society at large" which is composed of other mothers. I make this a distinct group because, I would argue, in many respects mothers constitute and inhabit what could be called a "culture of motherhood." Sixth is the extended family, and/or families of origin, surrounding the lesbian family. And finally is the created family, or the lesbian family itself.

In this list I have gone, generally, from those social bodies that are, in some sense, farthest from lesbian families (the state) to those who are the closest (other family members). This distinction between farthest and closest breaks down if we look too closely at it because, as mentioned, all these bodies constitute a web within which lesbian families exist and with which lesbian families interact, in some way, everyday. Nonetheless I want, in this paper, to focus on some of those bodies who are "closest to home," including immediate and extended family members, family friends, and other mothers. When we comprehend the struggles for identity and identification that occur at these levels, we begin to see some of the entry points for community and social services into these families and we also get an idea of some of the needs, issues and challenges that are unique to lesbian families.

THE SAMPLE

In 1992 I conducted over 30 interviews with lesbian mothers in Calgary and Edmonton, Alberta. There were two subsamples, each comprising approximately half the total sample. One of the subsamples contained six lesbian couples[1] who were raising children who had been conceived in prior heterosexual relationships. I will refer to these families as "blended families" and to the women in them as the "biological mother" and the "stepmother." This is not to suggest that these are necessarily the terms that these families and women use to describe themselves; we will see, in fact, that the inadequacy of language to accurately represent this family form is at the root of some of the challenges its members must face.

The second subsample contained six couples who were raising children who had been conceived within the lesbian relationships, generally through donor insemination. I refer to these as "donor insemination families" or "D. I. families" and to the women in them as "biological mother" and "non-biological mother."

There are actually five different means by which the women in my sample became mothers:

1. impregnation while in a lesbian relationship, either through donor insemination or sexual intercourse with a male;

2. being the partner of a woman who was impregnated while in a lesbian relationship;
3. impregnation via sexual intercourse while in a heterosexual relationship (generally a marriage);
4. becoming involved with a woman who had had a child or children while in a previous heterosexual relationship; and
5. becoming involved with a woman who had had a child while in a previous lesbian relationship.

Although only the third of the above routes to motherhood is consistent with "conventional" views regarding who a mother is, all the women in my sample were faced with the task of becoming mothers, in some sense, and all were faced with the challenge of exploring what motherhood can mean under these different circumstances. We will see that some of the challenges faced by lesbian mothers in the attempt to achieve the status of "mother" differ between the two types of family, often resulting in different experiences of family building and family life.

FAMILIES OF CREATION

In the immediate family, or family of creation, the people who are empowered to recognize someone as a mother are the adults and the children in the family. And it is at this level that we begin to see some marked differences between the donor insemination and blended families. Among the D. I. couples that I interviewed each woman considered herself "mother" and was considered "mother" by her partner. Thus, when asked, each woman was both the "mother" and the "other mother," although the terms "biological mother" and "non-biological mother" were often used to clarify who was being referred to. But the terms "biological mother" and "non-biological mother" did not differentiate the women in terms of their roles, tasks, and primacy of relationship with the child or children.

What was striking in these D. I. families was the extent to which all parenting tasks were shared by the couples. Frequently, for couples with young children, this meant the couple alternated part-time or seasonal jobs so that each would have equal mothering time. The women were equally invested in the mothering roles and equally oriented toward the children in a maternal manner. One of the biological mothers, Elly,[2] in a statement typical of the D. I. mothers, explained that

> The focus of the relationship is rearing our child and I don't even remember what that focus was before then. It's so, it sort of sweeps everything else away. You know, I think that will change as Astrid gets older and is more independent, but right now our world [revolves] around getting her up, getting her fed, getting her this, getting her that. She goes to bed, we have half an hour of exhausted talk and we fall together in bed exhausted. Our focus is on her. It has to be with young children. It just is, and I think that will change and I don't know what we'll discover our relationship to be when she's four or five. It's changed a lot, and a lot of that is really neat and cooperative. We share a lot of stuff together and we cooperate in zillions of ways, like I think Astrid is probably more co-parented than just about any other kid in the world. She's spent equal time with each of us. We equally do everything with her, like in terms of sharing responsibilities. The only thing that's different is I'm still nursing. So there's that cooperation, that mutual effort to survive that's there.

Iris, another D. I. mother, told me that she and her partner, Blaire, were working to minimize the differences between "biological mother" and "non-biological mother." She described those differences:

> Well, a lot of them are societally imposed, where people don't automatically call Blaire "mother" or don't automatically assume that Blaire, you know, changes the diapers or feeds him and stuff like that. Maybe even they assume that she takes on the father role, you know. So those types of impositions we try to diminish a lot . . . We're a parental unit and we're not divided by those distinctions, biological and non-biological.

In the D. I. families, each mother was equally primary to the child, and the couples often took pains not to exclude each other in any way. Iris described the importance of language in this respect:

> Blaire and I are both very careful to phrase everything properly. We always say it's "our" son because we're both so sensitive–it makes me sick–that if one of us said "It's my son" the other one

would go, "It's my son too." So we're very careful in how we word things, so that we include each other all the time that way.

The similarity in the roles played by the two mothers, brought up the problem of what term or name the women could use for themselves, and that could also be used by the children and others. Frequently, they felt that both being "mom" would be confusing and would dissolve them into some generic mothering entity with no individual identities. Many of the women felt that a child should have someone to call "mom" and this was usually the biological mother but the couples really struggled to come up with another term for the non-biological mother that was just as special and significant as "mom," rather than merely using her name. Unfortunately the English language is not very flexible when it comes to identifying, or even allowing the possibility of, two mothers for one child. Some couples settled on referring to each woman by name, and other couples called the biological mother "mom" and took their search for a name for the non-biological mother outside the bounds of the English language. Denise related the experiences that she and her partner, Wendy, had with this search:

> We tried to work on another term for me, something–"mother" in another language–that works well with English. Well, that doesn't work. We haven't found anything. And then I don't want him [their son, Bill] to just call me Denise. That's not special. I don't think that that is special enough. So right now when I talk to him now I call myself D. D. But the problem is that we're planning a second child, and I'm going to be that second child's bio-mother. So how do we have D. D. and W. W. [this works better with her real initials] and mom and mom? We haven't found a solution to that one yet. I don't know. I'm hoping Bill will help us with the solution. He's a very bright child–he's brilliant actually–so we're figuring that Bill will help us with it too [once he starts talking].

The search for names is also complicated by the fact that varying degrees of "closetedness" are required in different situations, although many of the women did not want one "reality" inside the home and another outside it. Elly described how she and Nancy dealt with this issue:

When Astrid was first born we made a joke that Nancy was the momma and I was the mooma because I was nursing. So for a long time we would be momma and mooma, and that was funny. We both call ourselves Astrid's mother. . . . She [Nancy] struggles with how she should identify herself with this child. Because if she says she's the mother she gets asked "how was the labor?" and "are you still nursing?" sorts of questions, and that's hard, so sometimes she says co-parent and sometimes she says mother and I think that's hard for her. But to everyone else, if we're ever saying anything, to people that we're out to, we say both mothers. At work I'm not out and so Nancy is my room-mate and she babysits Astrid.

In most of the donor insemination families that I interviewed the children were too young to be calling the mothers anything. Only two families had children who were four years or older. In these two families the children called the biological mother "mom" and the non-biological mother by her name. I was not able to interview the children at the time but, according to their mothers, they interacted with each woman similarly. These women were just their parents, and apart from the name thing, each was the child's mother. Linguistic limitations notwithstanding then, both of the women and the child or children in each of the D. I. families identified each woman as "moth-er," and identified their whole domestic group as a family.

In the blended families I found a very different situation. Some of the blended families were formed by two women who were already mothers but most were formed by one mother and one previously non-mothering woman. In these families it was striking that not only was there generally no name for the "step" mother, but frequently there was no clearly defined role for her either. One woman, Ellis, said that "it's really hard being in a relationship where you're the other adult but you're not the parent. It's a real tough role to play." Another woman, Barbara said that she felt that she had become "kind of an unidentified entity." She said "I call it no-name-brand parenting. You have . . . neither the role nor the definition nor the relationship."

In the blended families the children already had a mother who had probably been a single mother for some time. It was extremely diffi-cult for both the biological mothers and their children to determine what sort of parenting role a second woman would play in their families. Certainly bringing a stepfather into the family would also have been unsettling, but a conceptual space exists for the presence of a father or father-equivalent. Not so for a second mother. And while the introduction of a stepfather might require negotiating some of the fine details of his role and authority, his presence does not require that mothering, both the concept and the role as it has been played in the family, be completely renegotiated. But it is exactly this renegotiation of motherhood that the introduction of a second woman into the family requires.

Generally, the biological mothers had a great deal of difficulty sharing authority over the children with another woman. Laura, a biological mother, explained that "I sometimes get defensive around stuff with the kids and then suddenly Carol doesn't have authority where she thought she did, because I'm defensive or whatever. So it gets murky." Many of the stepmothers found that they had to watch that they did not overstep their boundaries. As Daphne explained:

> There's still the biological bond, and that overrides a lot. And when the partner, you know, the partner may know a lot, but there's still that fine line that you don't cross . . . It's been interesting for me because I've had to juggle just how much is my business and how much isn't.

For many stepmothers, the chief difficulty with not crossing the "fine line" was that the line, at the biological mother's discretion, always seemed to be shifting.

The biological mothers were not the only family members who experienced discomfort, at least initially, with attempts by their partners to play mothering roles. One of the biological mothers, Christine, illustrated a typical reaction of the children to the incoming partner. She said that she was unable to share parenting with her partner Janine because her son Nicki just wouldn't allow it. "And in some ways I wouldn't allow it either. He was mine and I wasn't prepared to share him with anybody. I had a complete set of ideas on how I wanted him raised, how he was going to be handled. And it really contradicted with how Janine viewed how children should be raised. And I think if we were to go back now I wouldn't change a whole lot what I did." In fact some of the stepmothers felt that they were not allowed to offer any input at all into how the children were raised. One woman said "you don't want to talk to mothers about their children. No matter

how good the relationship, you don't talk to them about their children.
I learned that the hard way."

Even when both of the women were biological mothers, they were
often unable to "cross-parent" and ended up clashing over parenting
styles. Janine explained that since she and Christine were both mothers they were:

> two authorities butting heads. . . . You know, I know best for my
> kids, you know best for your kids. Or [just] I know best. It's hard
> perhaps being in a relationship where both people think they
> know best. And certainly that's been an ongoing issue.

It was extremely difficult for these families to come together into
any sort of cohesive family unit. The biological mothers continued to
mother and their incoming partners tried to play a parental type of role
but often remained the unidentified "other" in the family. Different
family groups resolved these conflicts in different ways. Solutions
ranged from figuring out a way (sometimes with the help of a counsel-
lor or therapist) to co-parent to discarding the idea of co-parenting
altogether (meaning the children in any particular family were moth-
ered only by their biological mother and not her partner, regardless of
whether or not the partner was also a biological mother).

Thus we see a striking difference in the achievement of motherhood
within the blended and D. I. families. Whereas in D. I. families both
women are usually considered "mother" by all immediate family
members, in blended families, it is often only the biological mother
who is considered "mother" by all family members. Frequently there
is no consensus within the family regarding the role or the label of the
biological mother's partner; some family members, including herself,
may consider her "mother" while others do not–some may not even
consider her a member of the family. The complexity and conflict this
can bring to family life is a thread I will pick up shortly when considering the sorts of social and community services that would be useful
to lesbian families.

FAMILIES OF ORIGIN

When we move out from the immediate families to the families of
origin of the women in these couples, we see that things get more

complex for both the D. I. and the blended families. In the donor insemination families, generally the biological mother's parents and siblings acknowledged that she was indeed a mother, even if they were not happy with the circumstances under which she was mothering. The transition to motherhood, however, forced many women's parents and siblings to be more forthright in acknowledging and dealing with the lesbian relationship than they had been in the past. This was sometimes quite problematic. "As soon as a person comes out of the closet," Evelyn observed, "everybody around them goes into one." Some couples withdrew from their families during pregnancy to avoid hostility and conflict.

Although the biological mother's parents and siblings fully acknowledged the biological mother as a mother, their frequent discomfort with, and rejection of, the lesbian relationship (especially on the part of the parents) meant they often did not acknowledge the partner as a partner and almost definitely did not acknowledge or identify her as also a mother. Some of the biological mothers' families became quite involved in the pregnancy and occasionally very possessive of their daughter and grandchild. Their concerns about lesbian mothering were sometimes manifested in the form of an over-protectiveness that became intrusive or threatening to the lesbian couple. For example, Wendy's mother made it clear that if anything should happen to Wendy, Wendy's parents would try to take the baby away from Denise (because biologically the baby was *theirs*). This threat upset the couple tremendously, Wendy recalled:

> The whole time I was pregnant we were more concerned about what would happen if I was dead than concentrating on the fact that there was something fabulous happening here, you know. And I don't know, I sort of lived through the pregnancy with this morbid fear.

It took a great deal of time and effort to persuade Wendy's parents to acknowledge Denise as Bill's other parent, with equal parental rights.

It was considerably rarer for the non-biological mother's parents to see their daughter as a mother or to acknowledge the child as their grandchild. Often the non-biological mother's siblings were more willing to accept the self-identification of their sister. Nancy, a non-biological mother whose parents did not acknowledge either her partnership or her motherhood, offered a fairly typical statement regarding sibling relations:

> They [brothers] are really great, and my sister is a little bit more–she's not as willing to accept that we're actually lesbians. But that we can have a really great relationship together and stuff is okay with her, and that we're raising a kid together, that's fine. She can see Astrid as pretty close to like a niece, but I don't know if she's quite made that connection. It's pretty good with my siblings. They were great when we were there [visiting] and stuff.

In the blended families, the biological mother was already a mother and had long been recognized as such by her parents and siblings, but her family was unlikely to recognize her partner as a co-parent. The stepmother's family almost never acknowledged that their daughter (or sister) was playing a mothering role and were more likely to think that she was being exploited by a single mother who was using her for babysitting. Again we see many barriers to the stepmothers' quest to achieve the status of "mother"–some of the many barriers which lead some incoming partners to forfeit any claim to the status of mother in an attempt to keep some sort of peace and conceptual consistency within the family.

EXTENDED FAMILY RECONSIDERED

Most of the lesbian families had some sort of contact with their families of origin but, often, the issue of their lesbianism had created an emotional rift between them. In many cases, partly because of the difficult relationships they had with their families, the lesbian families were also geographically removed from their extended families. This emotional and geographical distance meant that for many lesbian families, it was actually their friends who constituted what they perceived to be their extended family.

The greatest amount of support, acknowledgement, and assistance generally came from friends, who as a result were often considered closer members of the families than were relatives. Friends of D. I. couples did not always start out with an understanding of why these couples wanted to have children but with a little education they usually came around. Each couple had a circle of friends, both lesbian and heterosexual, who offered enthusiastic support through the entire family-making process. Tina, a D. I. mother, noted how important friends can be:

> In our case both our families live some distance away, so we're not in regular contact with them. So really our circle of friends *is* the immediate family in that respect. And they probably are more important in our lives than if we were a heterosexual couple, because your whole lifestyle is, um, under attack–that's too strong a term–but is in question from the rest of society. [Whereas] everything you do as a heterosexual couple–as long as you don't put on a rubber suit and run around the neighborhood–is fine. There's no question that almost everything you do, because you are a lesbian, is called into question. So yeah, I think you're always looking to be, you know, bolstered by people who have the same kind of lifestyle or the same values that you do.

Nancy, another D. I. mother, concurred: "Our close friends really drew in and they became aunties. It's like it created an extended sort of family with a lot of our friends. Astrid has many aunties." Nancy's partner Elly elaborated on this, also pointing out the limitations of the friendship circle:

> [M]y close lesbian community [friends] I get quite a bit of support from. I had two years of diaper service paid for from all our friends, which is extraordinary. It's a large amount of money. It's like $1800 for two years of diaper service. People went together and paid for it. And I've had, I mean I happen to have a couple of more well-off friends and that, I mean they've bought tons of things for Astrid. Single lesbians without children, you know. Astrid loves them; they bring goodies all the time. So I have that, but that's sort of financial and some forms of other support but I don't . . . I don't feel like I have the support of any kind of community as much as I would if I was straight. In terms of just lifestyle support, you know, like young mothers with children getting together to do this. And I mean I have straight friends that have kids, but it's not the same as it would be if I had lesbian friends that had kids.

The extended family composed of friends was generally more supportive than many relatives of the maternal self-identities the women were struggling to establish and maintain, particularly in the D. I. families. In the blended families, however, the new "stepmothers" sometimes encountered in their friends skepticism and a reluctance to acknowledge them as mothers or parenting figures. Although most tried to find support within the lesbian community, a few encountered total incomprehension on the part of their lesbian friends as to why they would become part of a blended family. Furthermore, even though lesbian friends might have been willing to acknowledge that a family had been formed, and that there were difficulties maintaining it, they were sometimes hesitant to offer real assistance. Carol elaborated:

> One thing that we've noticed is people are quite willing to acknowledge how hard it is, you know, because we don't have enough money really to support our household, and that sort of thing. But nobody's really willing to get involved in that. You know, like, they're very much *our* children . . . Although they acknowledged how hard it must be for us, it was *our* problem. It was very much ours.

Nonetheless, many couples, in both the blended and D. I. families, reported that their friends, lesbian and heterosexual, were the closest they came to having an extended family.

Two important points should be noted here, both revolving around the fact that with lesbian families, it is often not immediately obvious who the various family members are. The first point is that immediate family members play decisive roles in identifying themselves and each other as family members with particular roles, and they do not always reach a consensus, especially within the blended families. Secondly, extended family members also play important roles in identifying and validating both the immediate family members and the very existence of a family. For lesbian families, however, the extended family is more often composed of friends than relatives, and all of this provides an important challenge to common notions of family based on blood or legal kinship.

As indicated earlier, immediate and extended family members are not the only "bodies" empowered to acknowledge and validate the status of mother. I will briefly consider one other such social body.

THE CULTURE OF MOTHERHOOD

It appeared to me, in the course of my research, that one of the key "players" involved in naming and identifying a woman's transition from woman to mother is other mothers. It appeared, in fact, that mothers occupy what could be called a "culture of motherhood" with its own entrance requirements, discourse, and possibly even epistemology. Other mothers start recognizing a woman as a mother when her pregnancy becomes apparent. This is aided by the "uniform" of pregnancy, maternity clothes, which I think are important symbolic indictors of a woman's shifting status.[3] Biological mothers in donor insemination families make this transition the same as heterosexual biological mothers do, but there is nothing to denote that their partners are also going through the same transition. Elly said, "I didn't know about this culture until I walked around pregnant. Women smile at you, talk about, you know, 'is it your first?', 'do you want a boy or a girl?', like out of the blue. It becomes women's, it's women's public domain." But the non-biological mothers often do not have a place in this domain.

This displacement becomes more pronounced as pregnancy progresses. For example, two of the couples spoke of an experience when they were in prenatal classes. They had each experienced their group being asked to split into mothers on one side of the room and fathers on the other. This left the non-biological mothers with nowhere to go. They were not welcomed into the group of mothers and although the fathers accepted them into their group they remained out of place. They were not, after all, fathers and their experiences were not identical to those of fathers.

The women spoke of an "inner circle" or "mommy's club" that only mothers enter. One of the mothers said "you sort of enter this mommy world, you know, and that's a whole other world. And you realize what you have in common with certain, with straight women, you have motherhood in common but somehow that denies some of your lesbianism so it's sort of a conditional relationship." Many of the women felt that their lesbianism marginalized them somewhat within the culture of motherhood but as long as they had given birth, they were generally accepted by other mothers as mothers. Again, the non-biological mothers were left out on two counts, their lesbianism and the fact that they did not appear to have a valid claim to the status of "mother." One of the biological mothers, Wendy, explained that:

> I know that Denise [her partner] felt particularly out of place and I got this impression from some of the women that it's like "well you've never had a child so what would you know?" kind of attitude. Women get really, not all women, but a lot of women get really righteous after they've gone through that, had a baby.

Whereas the non-biological mothers in donor insemination families had a great deal of difficulty making a place for themselves in the culture of motherhood, the stepmothers in the blended families generally did not even get anywhere near the culture of motherhood. Often they were denied, by both their partners and other mothers, any claim to the status of mother, even if they were performing mothering tasks and considered themselves a maternal or parental figure in the home.

An important component of the status of mother is a claim to maternal authority, something, as we have seen. the biological mothers in blended families often had some degree of difficulty sharing with their partners. Daphne, a stepmother in a blended family, expressed sentiments that were shared by all the stepmothers:

> Sometimes I feel left out. And sometimes it's just like being a kid and you're in the middle of it. Because Sharon is a mother, she goes into mother mode and I, I find that interesting. You know, you watch people that are mothers, and they have this "I know it all" approach. I watch with Laura and Carol [step-parenting friends], you know, and Laura knows it all and Carol and the kids know nothing. And I said one day "I often wonder just because someone biologically gives birth to a child, why all of a sudden it makes them the most knowledgeable person on everything under the sun, and the rest of us, until we give birth, don't really know anything."

It became evident, in the course of my research, that other mothers play a very important role in determining who can call themselves, and who can be called, "mother." Accompanying achievement of the status "mother" is entrance into the culture and discourse of motherhood, and this entrance is quite closely guarded.

A woman's lesbianism can marginalize her within the maternal discourse because here, as in most social spheres in Canada, there is an assumption of heterosexuality. To enter the discourse and offer information about herself and her life, a lesbian woman has to "come out" of a stigmatized closet. Although lesbianism does not exclude women from the discourse, it sometimes makes interaction there awkward. Those aspects of mothering that are unique to lesbian women have not been acknowledged in the mainstream, heterosexual maternal discourse. There, as elsewhere, lesbian women are rendered invisible by the assumption of universal heterosexuality.

Lesbian D. I. couples present a substantial challenge to established maternal culture by demanding that they (both partners) not be differentiated on the basis of having given birth. By insisting that non-biological mothers are mothers, too, these women have the potential to alter the understanding mothers have of motherhood. In this sense, lesbian motherhood through donor insemination can be seen as quite a revolutionary activity.

SOCIAL SERVICES/COMMUNITY SERVICES

One typical Sociology text gives "mother" as an example of an achieved status and explains that "a mother . . . cannot have that status unless and until she has a child"(Hagedorn, 1990, p. 41). My research reveals, however, that achieving the status of mother is nowhere near that simple, at least partly because what it means to "have a child" is not as clear as we often take it to be. To "have a child" or "be a mother" in the state's eyes requires one to give birth or adopt a child, and only one woman can be THE mother of any one child. But the state is not the only social body that is empowered to recognize some people as mothers. The church, the medical industry, society at large, friends, immediate and extended family, and other mothers also play central roles in determining who can and who cannot call themselves "mother."

Lesbian families are struggling on all these fronts for recognition but often victory in one arena is weakened by defeat in another. Negotiating their family and parental status, both within and outside their families, creates a dimension of family life for lesbians that heterosexual families generally do not experience in the same ways. It is the social marginalization, invisibility and stigmatization of lesbian families and lesbian mothers that render many of their family experiences different from those of heterosexuals. And those experiences and challenges that are unique to lesbian families[4] are almost always overlooked by mainstream family services and family-oriented organizations.

If we consider some of the social services typically available to families in Canada we can see some of these limitations. Parenting courses, for example, generally do not take into consideration the possibility that the parents might both be women and that this creates a different family dynamic than if the parents were male and female or even if there was just one parent, of either sex. Growing numbers of lesbian couples are having babies by donor insemination, but, still, the majority of lesbian families are those wherein the children were conceived in prior heterosexual relationships. As we have seen, blended lesbian families face many challenges in negotiating the familial roles of all family members and, in particular, the maternal roles of the women.

Other courses that are available for parents, for example self-esteem courses, dealing-with-teens courses, anger management courses, etc., also generally do not address the unique needs of lesbian families. It would be rare, for example, to find courses of this nature where there was an analysis of the heterosexist, patriarchal and misogynistic social context of lesbian families and a further analysis of how these factors might manifest themselves in terms of self-esteem, teen behavior, and anger.

State-sponsored homemakers, child-care workers, respite providers, foster-care providers and transition homes for abuse survivors also need to be sensitized to the unique experiences and needs of lesbian families. Even before this, however, they need to be made aware that such families exist. Just shifting away from the assumption of universal heterosexuality and dismantling heterosexism would go a long way toward supporting lesbian (and gay male) families.

Similarly, private community services and organizations that deal with the family need to be made aware of the existence of lesbian families, the sometimes unique dynamics of lesbian families, the challenges faced by lesbian families, and the role that they themselves (community services and organizations) play in defining "family" and recognizing and validating only some people as family members or as mothers. Grass-roots support groups, for example for parents of special-needs children, often reflect and propagate the social concepts of family based on heterosexual union and blood or legal kinship.

The changes that need to occur have to happen not just at the level of groups and services such as these but at all levels of society, since all are closely, sometimes reciprocally, related. This does not mean, however, that changes cannot begin at just one level. For example, state sponsored social services and private community services and groups could both acknowledge the existence of lesbian families, validate the identities of lesbian mothers, and try to meet some of the unique needs of lesbian families, even while the federal government does not yet allow the validation of lesbian relationships that legal marriage provides.

We must also consider the possibility that meeting the needs of lesbian families entails more than simply expanding and revising the programs and services that currently exist for families. Although it might be very useful, for example, if a parenting course took lesbian mothering experiences into consideration, perhaps what is really needed is a completely different type of course, or different format, or different service, to address the needs of lesbian mothers. Further research is required to answer this question and, in many ways, it is only the lesbian family members themselves who can answer it.

For the time being, given the resources and knowledge that we have, it is imperative to start bringing lesbian families out of the closet of ignorance that mainstream society maintains around them. We must reexamine our facile assumptions of who or what a mother is and who to designate as family members. We must be aware of, and sensitive to, the identity and legitimacy struggles lesbian mothers face everyday, both within their homes and outside them. Further, we need to be aware that just as there is no such thing as *"the* family" in Canada, there is also no such thing as "the lesbian family." In particular, blended lesbian families face some challenges and difficulties that are different from those faced by D. I. families, although both types of family share experiences resulting from existence in a heterosexist, patriarchal culture. And although I have not addressed this issue here, we must also be aware that lesbian single-mother families are not the same as heterosexual single-mother families, although they may have many concerns and experiences in common.

Lesbian mothers present a conceptual challenge, not only to others but also to themselves. They require that the state, the church, society, other mothers, etc., reconsider the criteria of the status of "mother." But even more, and on a daily basis, they require this reconsideration of themselves. Lesbian mothers are faced with the task of deconstructing motherhood in their own homes, inventing new language if necessary, and finding a new concept of motherhood that can capture the lesbian experience. Often these challenges are grappled with in the isolation of private homes and within individual families. Such isolation should not be necessary. It is time that mainstream understandings of "family" be substantially altered so that all family forms, including lesbian and gay male, that are outside the "traditional," heterosexual nuclear concept of family can also be understood as the families they are.

NOTES

1. Each subsample also contained a small number (a total of three) of single women, two of whom had *previously* been the non-biological mother or the step-mother in a lesbian family. The third woman was a single biological mother who identified herself as lesbian independent of involvement in a lesbian relationship. This paper focuses on the experiences of parenting couples.

2. All the participants' names given in this paper are pseudonyms.

3. As an aside, I think maternity clothes also serve the purpose of indicating that a woman has a "valid" reason for her increase in girth.

4. Some of the challenges involved in securing recognized parental and/or family status might also be experienced by gay male families. It is significant, however, that lesbian families are headed by two women, because they exist not only in a hetero-sexist social milieu but also in a patriarchal one.

REFERENCES

Dilapi, E. M. (1989) Lesbian mothers and the motherhood hierarchy. *Journal of Homosexuality*, 18 (1/2), 101-102.

Hagedorn, R. *Sociology* (4th ed.). (1990) Toronto: Holt, Rinehart and Winston of Canada, Limited.

Policy Alternatives
for a Diverse Community:
Lesbians and Family Law

Tricia Antoniuk

SUMMARY. While the legal position of lesbian mothers has improved over the past twenty years and some legal battles and human rights protection have been won, there is still a long way to go. This paper explores the acceptability of some policy alternatives within the lesbian community. Some of these alternatives are based on existing law as it has been applied to heterosexual families. For example, a number of the legal arguments have been used to defend the rights of step-parents who are not biological parents and yet have assumed a parenting role. The advantage of using such arguments is that there is already a legal precedent on which to build. The disadvantage is that the traditional family model may not be the model by which we wish to challenge the present legal context. Is equality contingent on equating lesbian families with traditional families, or is equality the acknowledgment and honouring of diversity and difference, with a legal system that is flexible enough to protect this diversity? These questions frame a debate within the lesbian community as well as within the larger polity. *[Article copies available for a fee from The Haworth Document Delivery Service: 1-800-342-9678. E-mail address: getinfo@haworthpressinc.com <Website: http://www.haworth pressinc.com>]*

KEYWORDS. Lesbian parents, family policy, equality rights, political dissent

Tricia Antoniuk, MSW, is affiliated with the Women's Resource Society of the Fraser Valley, P.O. Box 3044, Mission, B.C. V2V 4J3.

[Haworth co-indexing entry note]: "Policy Alternatives for a Diverse Community: Lesbians and Family Law." Antoniuk, Tricia. Co-published simultaneously *in Journal of Gay & Lesbian Social Services* (Harrington Park Press, an imprint of The Haworth Press, Inc.) Vol. 10, No. 1, 1999, pp. 47-60; and: *Queer Families, Common Agendas: Gay People, Lesbians, and Family Values* (ed: T. Richard Sullivan) Harrington Park Press, an imprint of The Haworth Press, Inc., 1999, pp. 47-60. Single or multiple copies of this article are available for a fee from The Haworth Document Delivery Service [1-800-342-9678, 9:00 a.m. - 5:00 p.m. (EST). E-mail address: getinfo@haworthpressinc.com].

From the outset it is important to acknowledge that there is no consensus within the lesbian community itself about how to proceed in the struggle for legal recognition. Some of the policy and legal implications are indeed complex. Some would argue that equal status with heterosexual couples and families is a positive step, protected in the Canadian Human Rights Act, while others would argue that this type of equal status is detrimental, since it only perpetuates patriarchal and hierarchical structures that have been oppressive of women.

As Nancy Polikoff (1990) points out, one of the difficulties is that current definitions of family are based on the traditional nuclear family model:

> Two theories underlying the legal definitions of parent and non-parent deny the existence of nontraditional families. The first theory is that every child should have one mother and one father, neither more nor less. The second theory is that those two persons identified as mother and father should have all the rights and responsibilities of parenthood, whereas nonparents should have none. (Polikoff, 1990, p. 468)

By their very existence, lesbian families (and other nontraditional families) challenge these basic assumptions, which have been the foundation of most family law.

POLICY ALTERNATIVES

Legal Arguments that Recognize the Parent Role

In cases involving lesbian parents which have been reported in legal journals, the following arguments have been used to defend the role of the non-biological lesbian mother as a significant parental figure in a child's life.

De facto Parenthood

"A de facto parent is 'that person who, on a day-to-day basis, assumes the role of parent, seeking to fulfill both the child's physical needs and his psychological need for affection and care' " (*Nancy S. v.*

Michele G., 1991, p. 555). While de facto parent status does recognize the relationship of a child to a non-biological parent, it does not give that parent the right to custody unless the biological parent is considered unsuitable as a parent to the child.

> . . . the cases establish that nonparents, even if they qualify as "de facto parents," may be recognized in guardianship or dependency proceedings and may even obtain custody over children with whom they have established a relationship, but that custody can be awarded to a de facto parent *only* if it is established by clear and convincing evidence that parental custody is detrimental to the children. (*Nancy S. v. Michele G.*, 1991, p. 555)

In other words, de facto parenthood has not been used to extend legal recognition to persons who have fulfilled a parent role in addition to the role of a competent biological parent. So while the definition itself could certainly apply to a non-biological lesbian mother, in case law it has not been interpreted to recognize co-parent rights to access or to joint custody.

In loco Parentis

"In the context of torts, the concept of in loco parentis has been used to impose upon persons standing 'in loco parentis' the same rights and obligations imposed by statutory and common law upon parents" (*Nancy S. v. Michele G.*, 1991, p. 556). In other words, this status gives the non-biological parent the same rights as a biological parent.

Polikoff (1990) discusses the strengths and weaknesses of the in loco parentis doctrine:

> On the one hand, courts concerned with the best interests of children are unwilling to ignore the importance of parental relationships children develop with those who are not their legal parents. On the other hand, courts apply the in loco parentis doctrine selectively because literal application of the doctrine provides no protection for the rights of legal parents. . . . The rights and responsibilities of parenthood under this doctrine are based on the reality of who intentionally fulfills the parenting function, not on the one-mother/one-father model. (Polikoff, 1990, p. 506-507)

This legal doctrine could be used to recognize the parental role of non-biological lesbian parents, in a similar way that it has been used in the courts to recognize the rights of step-parents. However, in practice courts have refused to use this doctrine to apply to lesbian families, and have justified this by relying on the recognition of legal marital status before applying in loco parentis (Kovacs, 1995, p. 524).

The advantage of in loco parentis is that it is meant to recognize the family and parental figures as they exist in the child's life, not according to some external definition of family. However, in reality we know that judiciary discretion has nonetheless used a traditional definition of family to exclude lesbians and thereby discriminate against lesbian families.

In May 1996 the Canadian Human Rights Act was amended to include sexual orientation as grounds for which discrimination is prohibited. Given this governmental mandate of not discriminating based on sexual orientation, legal arguments such as in loco parentis which have relied on traditional definitions of family may be challenged to be interpreted in a non-discriminatory manner. It will be very important to follow how the Canadian Human Rights Act concretely affects judiciary ruling involving family law. The Human Rights Act could provide the legal basis for appealing decisions which appear to be based on discrimination.

Equitable Estoppel

"The doctrine of equitable estoppel 'would make it possible for non-legal parents to prevent the legal parent from claiming in court that only the legal relationship between him or her and the child should be recognized'" (Kovacs, 1995, p. 516).

In other words, if the legal parent claims that the relationship between the non-legal parent and the child should not be legally recognized, this allows the legally unrecognized parent to argue for their status as parent. Nancy Polikoff explains it like this:

> Functional parents–including lesbian parents–may develop a parent-child relationship in several ways. A lesbian-mother family can hold itself out as including two mothers. It can treat a child as part of both mothers' extended families. A child can have the last names of both mothers. . . . A legally unrecognized mother can contribute to the child's financial support and the legally recog-

nized mother can accept such payment. A written or oral agreement can exist between the two women that they will jointly rear the child. Under any of these circumstances, the legally unrecognized mother should be able to seek the legal status of parent. She should be permitted to assert that by creating the parent-child relationship and representing that child rearing was a joint endeavor, the legally recognized mother has been estopped from denying the functional parent the status of legal parent. (Polikoff, 1990, p. 499)

Equitable Parenthood

"The doctrine of equitable parenthood differs from equitable estoppel in that the latter is 'limited to providing specific relief in a specific action,' while the former 'establishes legal parenthood' " (Kovacs, 1995, p. 521). Kovacs argues that while this status has not been used to support gay/lesbian families, the definition would be compatible with the experience of many gay and lesbian families.

While the equitable parenthood doctrine, as expressed by the *Atkinson* court, is expressly limited to a "husband" and "a child born or conceived during the marriage," it is unlike the presumption of legitimacy, in that the crucial issue is the development of a parent-child relationship. The reasoning could therefore extend to gay/lesbian families where the second parent is held responsible for child support. (Kovacs, 1995, p. 523)

Polikoff (1990) states that "establishing legal parenthood decreases the likelihood of future litigation, which, by its nature, is detrimental to the child's best interests" (p. 501).

This is an important point which could provide a guideline to unite the various perspectives in the lesbian community. While there is a fear of and resistance to pursuing legal recognition of lesbian families by some members of the lesbian community, ultimately we know that the absence of any legal recognition has not generally been in the child's best interests. Establishing legal parenthood is one way of recognizing the parental relationships which reflect the child's reality, as well as protecting those parental relationships in the case of dissolution of the lesbian family.

Definitions of Parenthood

The preceding legal arguments depend to some degree on a traditional definition of parenthood. It has therefore been proposed that the definition of parenthood needs to be changed to account for the realities of children's lives, that is, to include non-traditional families, of which lesbian families are only one example. Both Katharine Bartlett and Nancy Polikoff have proposed ways in which the definition of parenthood could be altered to be more inclusive (Kovacs, 1995, p. 527).

> Rather than emphasizing the children's interests in the continuity and stability of their parental relationships, current definitions of parenthood emphasize the state's interest in preserving the fiction of family homogeneity. Thus, courts should redefine parenthood to include anyone in a functional parental relationship that a legally recognized parent created with the intent that an additional parent-child relationship exist. (Polikoff, 1990, p. 573)

The legal profession, taking advantage of the absence of legal status of non-biological parents, has used the following argument:

> . . . expanding the definition of a "parent" in the manner advocated by appellant could expose other natural parents to litigation brought by child-care providers of long standing, relatives, successive sets of step-parents or other close friends of the family. No matter how narrowly we might attempt to draft the definition, the fact remains that the status of individuals claiming to be parents would have to be litigated and resolution of these claims would turn on elusive factual determinations of the intent of the natural mother, the perceptions of the children, and the course of conduct of the party claiming parental status. (*Nancy S. v. Michele G.*, 1991, p. 558)

Nancy Polikoff counters their argument in this way:

> The children born to the families whose cases are discussed here have two mothers who willingly participated in their conception and birth, and who openly raised them as coparents. If any of the biological mothers can prove it is in the best interests to deny

contact between the child and the other mother, she should litigate the case on that basis. Attempting to avoid such litigation on the merits by equating the nonbiological mother's legal status with that of a babysitter or family friend does not demonstrate a principled defense of either parental rights or the best interests of children. Rather, the technique is a bad faith assertion of a definition of parenthood that is no longer adequate to recognize contemporary family forms. (Polikoff, 1990, p. 542)

Polikoff (1990) argues strongly that it is important to "distinguish between categories of third-party claimants" (p. 513) since this will acknowledge the realities of children's lives who live in nontraditional families.

The purpose of distinguishing among categories of third-party visitation claimants is to recognize the explicitly parental status that some "third parties" occupy in the lives of children. Once "third parties" achieve such status, courts should seek to continue the parent-child relationship regardless of what happens to the adult relationship. (Polikoff, 1990, p. 521)

An example of how the definition of parent has been changed to include same-sex couples occurred recently in British Columbia. In July 1997 the Family Relations Act was amended (Bill 31) to include the following definition of spouse: A spouse is someone who "lived with another person in a marriage-like relationship for a period of at least 2 years . . . and, for the purposes of this Act, the marriage-like relationship may be between persons of the same gender."

Limitations of Legal Arguments

While the above principles could be used in the legal system to establish parental rights and to fight for access and custody, one of the problems of this approach is that it must be settled in a legal fashion. As argued by Kovacs (1995): "Requiring gay/lesbian couples to go to court to seek validation of their relationships with their children undermines their search for autonomy and the freedom to define their own personal relationships" (p. 530-531).

Also, the presence of discrimination in the courts is evident, so relying on legal judgments leaves lesbians extremely vulnerable. Lesbians may be hesitant to enter the legal system at all, given the patriarchal and hierarchical patterns that have been perpetuated there. "The stress of entering the legal system and potentially submitting the family to evaluation according to standards rooted in homophobia and heterosexism is as much a deterrent as the uncertainty of asserting untested legal theories" (Polikoff, 1990, p. 526).

Probably most lesbians would argue that some degree of legal protection is worth fighting for; however, this battle is a two-edged sword, as pointed out by Karen Andrews (1995). When she argued for health benefits to be expanded to include her same-sex partner, she won the right to have benefits, but the definition was changed so that it did not include the recognition of the nature of the relationship:

> It was simply too much for a court or government to acknowledge my life in any kind of bureaucratic or legislative way so they redesigned the whole thing such that we all got a better result: gay and lesbian households disappeared, but so did everybody else's. (Andrews, 1995, p. 366)

Some lesbians would argue that changing such definitions to be broad and non-specific in terms of the nature of the relationship is the best way to prevent discrimination. This allows diversity and inclusivity, and does not require any justification or defense regarding the exact nature of the relationship. On the other hand, lesbians have experienced invisibility as an effective tool in being silenced and not having our relationships acknowledged.

Essentially we must consider both of these issues seriously. Definitions which are broad and non-discriminatory can benefit all marginalized groups. However, there are situations in which remaining invisible can be detrimental, and specific acknowledgment can be critical. A good example of this is having sexual orientation included in the Canadian Human Rights Act so that discriminatory practices can be challenged.

Legal Recognition of Same-Sex Marriage

Kathryn Kovacs (1995) argues that the legal recognition of same-sex marriage is the best way to address the present inequalities of the legal system. If the relationship of the lesbians themselves is recognized, this allows a recognized structure by which family law can apply to same-sex couples. In other words, children would be born into a recognized family unit that would automatically provide rights and responsibilities to both parents, without having to turn to the legal system for recognition.

> Legalizing gay/lesbian marriage would enable less intrusive and more predictable resolution of family disputes. "If states licensed same-sex marriage, the courts could use precedents from marriage and family law to determine the legal rights of members of same-sex families." (Kovacs, 1995, p. 538)

She also argues that there are precedents in heterosexual family law that recognize the rights of a marital family over the rights of a biological father. This could support lesbians who use alternative insemination and who fear that the biological rights of the father can override the day-to-day parenting relationship of the same-sex partner. It could also allow a lesbian family to be seen as providing stability and security for a child, rather than portraying it as a perversion or a detriment in custody arrangements.

> The greatest benefit of legalizing gay/lesbian marriage is that it strikes at the heart of homophobia by instructing society that gay/lesbian families are entitled to the protection and recognition of the legal system and the respect of us all. (Kovacs, 1995, p. 539)

Recognition of same-sex marriage within the lesbian community is somewhat controversial however. While some lesbians see this as a logical extension of equality rights, others feel that the recognition of same-sex marriage is a backwards step into the oppressive and regulative aspect of marriage. It could, for example, reinforce domestication and monogamy (Robson, 1992, p. 126). Didi Herman (1989) expands on this notion:

> Our reliance on the language of monogamy, cohabitation, life-long commitment, and other essentials of bona fide heterosexual couple-dom may divide us, not only from other lesbians and gays who do not live in this fashion, but from all people defined as "single" by virtue of their exclusion from the model. . . . By claiming our rights as spouses, rather than our rights/needs as people, we emulate and legitimize the ideological norm and we also compound the marginalization of others. (Herman, 1989, p. 797 & 799)

This highlights again the double-edge sword effect of many efforts to gain legal recognition. While legal protection and non-discrimination are generally worth fighting for, the system itself is oppressive, and there is no guarantee that the legal protection which will be received will be emancipatory. "The necessities of conforming to the norms of legal argumentation may lead to the holding of unintended and potentially reactionary positions" (Herman, 1989, p. 808). Herman goes on to argue:

> Analogies are problematic: they require a simplification that inhibits an understanding of complexities and contradictions. But legal discourse is all about categorization, finding similar facts, and treating likes alike. (Herman, 1989, p. 814)

This is best illustrated by the legal arguments used to gain custody for lesbian parents in court battles. Successful legal arguments are predicated on demonstrating how lesbian mothers are similar to heterosexual mothers, that is, how they can provide a healthy environment similar to that which a heterosexual mother can. If a mother is seen to deviate from this norm, she risks losing custody or facing charges for change of custody. Her argument that an alternative lifestyle will be healthier for the child in the long run is not one which courts up until now have been open to consider. The pervasiveness of heterosexuality is ultimately a tricky battle to fight.

Legal Right of Same-Sex Parents to Adopt

The right for both parents in same-sex couples to legally adopt a child is another approach that has been proposed. This gives legal status to both parents in a lesbian relationship and can apply to different lesbian family constellations. For example, a non-biological lesbian partner can apply to adopt the children of her partner's heterosexual relationship, a non-biological lesbian partner can apply to adopt the child of her partner who has used alternative insemination, or the two lesbian partners can apply as a couple to adopt a child.

This possibility has recently been legally mandated in British Columbia (Adoption Act, November 1996), and it makes the law in British Columbia among the most progressive in the world regarding the adoption of children. It gives both lesbian parents legal rights as parents, and no longer forces one of them to have sole legal parental rights.

Since this law is so recent, it is difficult to evaluate the effects that it will have on the legal rights of lesbian parents and on custody and access disputes. However, it is progressive in that it gives both parents at least some ground to stand on if there are any legal challenges which arise.

Nancy Polikoff (1990) has argued that not only should lesbian parents both be allowed to adopt, but that they should be able to do this without the termination of existing parental rights:

> Consistent with the premises of this article, adoption without termination of parental rights should be available if all existing parents consent. Courts and legislatures should permit such adoptions without considering the number or gender of the resulting parents. This change in the law would provide parents with an indisputable method of establishing parental rights. It would also permit parents to structure legal families that reflect their actual families. (Polikoff, 1990, p. 524)

In other words, if a father from a previous marriage wanted to retain parental rights for his children, this would not prevent a lesbian partner from adopting these same children if she is acting in the capacity of a functional parent with their biological mother.

While the option of co-parent adoption gives legal rights to the same-sex couple as parents, it does not directly acknowledge their relationship as a couple. This is an effective way of rendering lesbian families invisible, as already highlighted in the fight by Andrews (1995) for same-sex spousal benefits. In a similar fashion to the Andrews case, although the parental relationships of the two adults are acknowledged, their relationship as spouses or partners does not legally exist. Again, some lesbians will see this as positive, allowing lesbians themselves to define their own relationships, while others will feel that this is just another way that lesbian relationships are legally "invisible."

Same-sex co-parent adoption will still require involvement with the legal system and submission to its adjudicatory function, a submission to which some lesbians are resistant: "It will continue to be the case that the court will be required to determine whether the adoption is in the best interest of the child" (Findlay, 1995, p. 40). However, it will involve the legal system at a point when the lesbian family is establishing itself as a family, not at a time when there are problems or disputes that require legal judgments. This allows lesbian families to be legally recognized as stable and healthy, rather than relying on judiciary discretion in custody battles which has tended to have strong heterosexist biases.

CONCLUSION

Slow progress is being made in policy and legislation regarding lesbians. This has been the result of many court battles and improved human rights protection of lesbians and gay men. However, with regards to family law, cases are often regarded in isolation, and women who are open about their lesbian identity and relationships are still discriminated against on a regular basis. As Nancy Polikoff states: "The courtroom is no place in which to affirm our pride in our lesbian sexuality, or to advocate alternative child-rearing designed to produce strong, independent women" (as cited in Arnup, 1995, p. 383).

One of the biggest difficulties in the lesbian community's confrontation with family law derives from the irresolution of the legal status of the same-sex, non-biological parent. In some cases, lesbians have used the ambivalence of existing laws against each other, occasioning bitter internal community disputes.

> The legal system provides boundaries for the rest of society which it does not provide lesbians and gay men–boundaries to limit unconscionable acts, and boundaries to define and support families. . . . Not only are we denied the legal protections and support our families need, we also can't rely on the predictability the law provides. And so, when we're angry, we go to court and take sometimes extreme positions. We use the laws we hate against each other, or we are forced to distort our family to fit the limited legal definitions available to us. (National Center for Lesbian Rights, 1991, p. 562)

So although some lesbians are reluctant to fight for legal recognition and rights, which they believe will imply conformity and submission to heterosexual norms, it is apparent that a lack of legal recognition and rights provides no protection for lesbians who end up in court. Didi Herman (1989) argues that: "Perhaps we need to retreat from an either/or position. Rights, like family, mean different things to different people" (p. 809). We need to recognize where rights claims are strategic and empowering, as well as working for more fundamental societal change and a greater acknowledgment of diversity in relationships and families (Herman, 1989).

It is important to understand that legal recognition of the "functional" family, that is, the family as it exists in reality, is the best way to protect children and their parents, instead of forcing them to try to fit into definitions of family which do not reflect their reality. Children need us to protect their best interests and honour their most significant relationships by legally recognizing their families even when they do not conform to the traditional family model (Polikoff, 1990). This means that both socially and legally we must acknowledge the existence of lesbian families, understand the various ways that lesbian families are formed, and affirm the stability and benefits that lesbian families can provide to children.

REFERENCES

Andrews, K. (1995). Ancient affections: Gays, lesbians & family status. In K. Arnup (Ed.), *Lesbian parenting: Living with pride & prejudice* (pp. 358-377). Charlottetown, P.E.I.: gynergy books.

Arnup, K. (1987). "Mothers just like others": Lesbians, divorce, and child custody in Canada. *Canadian Journal of Women and the Law, 3*, 18-32.

Arnup, K. (1995). Living in the margins: Lesbian families & the law. In K. Arnup (Ed.), *Lesbian parenting: Living with pride & prejudice* (pp. 378-398). Charlottetown, P.E.I.: gynergy books.

B.C. Ministry for Children and Families. (1996). *Adoption Act* [On-line]. Available: http://www.qp.gov.bc.ca/stat_reg/statutes/00500.htm.

Brophy, J. (1991). New families, judicial decision-making, and children's welfare. *Canadian Journal of Women and the Law, 5*, 484-497.

Brown, H.C. (1992). Lesbians, the state and social work practice. In M. Langan & L. Day (Eds.), *Women, oppression and social work: Issues in anti-discriminatory practice* (pp. 201-219). London: Routledge.

Eaton, M. (1990). Lesbians and the law. In S.D. Stone (Ed.), *Lesbians in Canada* (pp. 109-132). Toronto: Between the Lines.

Findlay, B. (1995). *All in the family values: An examination of the construction of "family" and the impact of law on the lives of lesbians and gay men.* Unpublished paper.

Flaks, D.K. (1994). Gay and lesbian families: Judicial assumptions, scientific realities. *William and Mary Bill of Rights Journal, 3:1*, 345-372.

Gross, W.L. (1986). Judging the best interests of the child: Child custody and the homosexual parent. *Canadian Journal of Women and the Law, I*, 505-531.

Herman, D. (1989). Are we family?: Lesbian rights and women's liberation. *Osgoode Hall Law Journal, 28(4)*, 789-815.

Kovacs, K.E. (1995). Recognizing gay and lesbian families: Marriage and parental rights. *Law and Sexuality, 5,* 513-539.

McMackon, B. (1995). *Child welfare policy: Lesbian custody issues.* Unpublished paper.

Nancy S. v. Michele G., 279 Cal. Rptr. 212 (Ct. App. 1991). In W.B. Rubenstein (Ed.). (1993). *Lesbians, gay men, and the law* (pp. 554-560). New York: The New Press.

National Center for Lesbian Rights. (1991-92). Our day in court–against each other: Intra-community disputes threaten all of our rights. In W.B. Rubenstein (Ed.). (1993). *Lesbians, gay men, and the law* (pp. 561-562). New York: The New Press.

Patterson, C.J. (1992). Children of lesbian and gay parents. *Child Development, 63,* 1025-1042.

Patterson, C.J. (1994). Children of the lesbian baby boom: Behavioral adjustment, self-concepts, and sex role identity. In B. Greene & G.M. Herek (Eds.), *Psychological perspectives on lesbian and gay issues: Vol. 1. Lesbian and gay psychology: Theory, research, and clinical applications* (pp. 156-175). Thousand Oaks, CA: Sage.

Patterson, C.J. (1995). Adoption of minor children by lesbian and gay adults: A social science perspective. *Duke Journal of Gender Law & Policy* [On-line]. Available: http://www.law.duke.edu/journals/djglp/djgv2a11.htm.

Pershing, S.B. (1994). "Entreat me not to leave thee": *Bottoms v. Bottoms* and the custody rights of gay and lesbian parents. *William and Mary Bill of Rights Journal, 3:1,* 289-325.

Pies, C. (1985). *Considering parenthood: A workbook for lesbians.* San Francisco: Spinsters Ink.

Polikoff, N. (1990). This child does have two mothers: Redefining parenthood to meet the needs of children in lesbian-mother and other nontraditional families. *The Georgetown Law Journal, 78,* 459-575.

Robson, R. (1992). *Lesbian (out)law: Survival under the rule of law.* Ithaca, NY: Firebrand Books.

Rubenstein, W.B. (Ed.). (1993). *Lesbians, gay men, and the law.* New York: The New Press.

Tataryn, J., Timberg, T., & Desjarlais, N.C. (1996). *Same sex, same laws: Lesbians, gay men, and the law in B.C.* Vancouver: Legal Services Society.

Victoria Status of Women Action Group. (1993). *The legal status of lesbians in British Columbia.* Vancouver: Legal Services Society.

Weston, K. (1991). *Families we choose: Lesbians, gays, kinship.* New York: Columbia University Press.

Yogis, J.A., Duplak, R.R., & Trainor, J.R. (1996). *Sexual orientation and Canadian law: An assessment of the law affecting lesbian and gay persons.* Toronto: Emond Montgomery Publications Ltd.

Raising Our Sons:
Gay Men as Fathers

Jerry J. Bigner

SUMMARY. Gay men become fathers for a variety of reasons. The research literature on the parenting abilities and styles of gay fathers is examined and compared with that of non-gay fathers. Particular attention is given to the idea of gay fathers raising sons in relation to cultural stereotypes about homosexual men and gender role development and identity. Rather than promoting traditional masculine role development among sons, gay fathers may offer their children the advantage of serving as a model of androgyny. The benefits offered in this regard to children are discussed in relation to long-term life span development of children. Children of gay fathers also benefit by learning about the insidious nature of homophobic and heterosexist attitudes. By disclosing their sexual orientation and lifestyle to children, gay fathers help children to learn the importance of tolerance and the necessity of respecting individual differences in others. *[Article copies available for a fee from The Haworth Document Delivery Service: 1-800-342-9678. E-mail address: getinfo@haworthpressinc.com <Website: http://www.haworthpressinc.com>]*

KEYWORDS. Gay fathers, life span development, androgyny, tolerance, heterosexism

The notion of gay men as parents is one of the major drivers fueling homophobic and heterosexist attitudes that are used to prevent or

Jerry J. Bigner, PhD, is Professor, Department of Human Development and Family Studies, Colorado State University, Ft. Collins, CO 80523.

[Haworth co-indexing entry note]: "Raising Our Sons: Gay Men as Fathers." Bigner, Jerry J. Co-published simultaneously in *Journal of Gay & Lesbian Social Services* (Harrington Park Press, an imprint of The Haworth Press, Inc.) Vol. 10, No. 1, 1999, pp. 61-77; and: *Queer Families, Common Agendas: Gay People, Lesbians, and Family Values* (ed: T. Richard Sullivan) Harrington Park Press, an imprint of The Haworth Press, Inc., 1999, pp. 61-77. Single or multiple copies of this article are available for a fee from The Haworth Document Delivery Service [1-800-342-9678, 9:00 a.m. - 5:00 p.m. (EST). E-mail address: getinfo@haworthpressinc.com].

minimize custody and parental rights to homosexual parents. This stereotypic idea, held by many people in society, suggests that gay men cannot possibly serve as appropriate sex-role models of masculinity for children, especially boys. It also suggests that gay men who function as caregivers for children will ultimately sexually molest and abuse them, and that boys are especially vulnerable to such maltreatment. The very idea, even, of being a parent who also is gay is confusing, contradictory, and inconsistent with the stereotypical image many people hold of gay men. Even among the gay community, those men who are parents are often seen and sometimes treated as pariahs because they do not fit in with the mainstream gay culture. This culture is singles-oriented, and children are not typically included in the idealized image of what necessarily constitutes a gay family.

Yet, in spite of such negativity associated with gay parenthood, it is estimated that about 20 to 25 percent of self-identified gay men are also fathers (Bell & Weinberg, 1978; Bozett & Sussman, 1989; Maddox, 1982; Miller, 1979b; Weinberg & Williams, 1974). This group of gay men who are also fathers constitutes a minority within a minority in our culture. It is impossible, however, to estimate the actual number of gay men who are parents because many are married to women or remain "closeted" for other reasons.

There are myriad reasons that may explain why gay men become parents (Barret & Robinson, 1990; Bigner & Bozett, 1989; Bigner & Jacobsen, 1989a, b; Bozett, 1987a). These may be particular to an individual and comprise a complex of motivations. Research and clinical observation suggest that three broad trends may play a role in this regard:

1. It is thought that the majority of gay men who have become fathers experienced a delayed coming-out process because of the negative stigmas associated with homosexuality promoted by our homophobic culture and especially by families and peer groups that value heterosexism (Bigner, 1996). They entered into heterosexual marriages without either fully accepting their sexual orientation or remained in denial about this for a number of years. Some sincerely desired to have a healthy, successful marriage with a woman in which they hoped for or managed for some time to ignore or not act upon their homosexual feelings (Barret & Robinson, 1990; Bigner & Jacobsen, 1989a, b; Miller, 1979a, b). Others were fully aware of their sexual orientation but

entered heterosexual marriage for various reasons that resemble those of non-gay men. Regardless, internalized homophobia can be largely responsible for promoting a charade of heterosexuality for most of these gay fathers. It is believed that the midlife transition experiences of intense self-examination (Levinson, 1986) coupled with the toll exacted by an ill-fitting lifestyle as a heterosexual serve as trigger events for initiating the developmental changes associated with the coming-out process. These facilitate coming out at some point usually following years of heterosexual marriage and the birth of children. Most marriages typically end in divorce upon disclosure and the men, their children, and former spouses encounter the adjustments involved (Hays & Samuels, 1989). With much assistance from therapy and support groups, newly emergent gay fathers embark upon a new developmental path in establishing this personal identity.

2. Other gay fathers follow a different developmental path than that just described. These men willfully choose to become a father by establishing arrangements and relationships with either a lesbian and/or her partner or with a heterosexual woman. In most instances, conception usually occurs via artificial insemination. Some marriages commence with the woman's full awareness of the man's homosexual or bisexual orientation beforehand. It has become more apparent as an increasing number of lesbians and gay men become involved in parental liaisons that there are legal arrangements to be made before a conception occurs. It is important to arrange the agreements regarding custody, visitation, and support on the part of each party involved.

3. In general, there is little difference between gay and non-gay fathers in their desire for children (Bigner & Jacobsen, 1989a). Both cite the desire for nurturing children, for the constancy of children in their lives, to achieve some means of immortality via children, and for the sense of family that children help to provide. However, gay fathers place greater emphasis on the notion that parenthood impacts adult status in the eyes of the community-at-large which may be a disguised form of internalized homophobia, i.e., parenthood is a connotation of heterosexuality and this status may have once served a protective function in their denial of homosexuality.

PARENTING BY GAY FATHERS

It has been clearly established by a number of investigations using a variety of measurement methods that sexual orientation of an adult is an invalid variable in determining the ability to parent children and provide for their care effectively (Bailey et al., 1995; Barret & Robinson, 1990; Benkov, 1994; Bigner, 1996; Bigner & Bozett, 1989; Bigner & Jacobsen, 1989a; Bozett, 1987, 1989; Bozett & Sussman, 1989; Flaks et al., 1995; Gottman, 1989; Patterson, 1992, 1994, 1995; Turner, Scadden, & Harris, 1990; Strickland, 1995). Homosexual orientation of fathers, mothers, or other caregivers has never been proven to be a detriment to the welfare of children they rear.

When investigators have examined parenting styles and behaviors of gay fathers, they are consistently found to be similar to heterosexual fathers in many respects (Barret & Robinson, 1990; Bigner, 1996; Bigner & Jacobsen, 1989a; Bozett, 1987, 1989; Bozett & Sussman, 1989; Patterson, 1992, 1994, 1995). When differences are noted, the distinguishing factors tend to depict gay fathers in a positive manner in comparison with heterosexual fathers (Barret & Robinson, 1990; Bigner & Bozett, 1989; Bozett & Sussman, 1989). For example, gay fathers have been found to be more astute to children's needs, more nurturant in providing caregiving, and less traditional than heterosexual fathers who typically perceive their principle parenting function to be that of provider. Gay fathers are repeatedly described in studies as having warm and positive relationships with their children (Patterson, 1992). The home lives and environments they provide for children are consistently described as stable and highly structured. When compared with heterosexual fathers, gay fathers are found to be more strict with children but not authoritarian. Instead, they appear to conform to an authoritative parenting style that emphasizes the use of reasonable limits on children's behavior while facilitating their ability to make choices.

Why is a father's sexual orientation irrelevant to his parenting abilities and performance? There has been an increased call over the last three decades for men to become more involved in childrearing and in other parental duties (Benokraitis, 1996; Bigner, 1972). The expectation of men in their contemporary parenting role is to learn how to function with a less traditional orientation and with more of an androgynous approach. Men today are expected to include more nurturant and expressive aspects of their behavior not only in raising children but in relating with spouses. Gay fathers, especially those who have a history of a heterosexual marriage, are likely to have had experience with these androgynous notions and expectations for their behavior as males similar to heterosexual fathers (Bigner, 1996). However, gay fathers may be more comfortable in relationships with children and women than heterosexual men (Bigner & Bozett, 1989). In examining the research about their parenting styles and behaviors, gay fathers appear to incorporate a greater degree of emotional expressiveness and less reliance on traditional sex-role behaviors leading to more nurturant relationships with children as compared with heterosexual fathers (Bigner & Jacobsen, 1989a, b).

In speculating about why this is so, it is possible to surmise that gay males most likely recognized themselves and were recognized by others as being different from other males in their family of origin. Their interests, behavior, thoughts, and other attributes distinguished them from other males such as fathers and brothers, for example, who were more likely to have lives, behaviors, and attitudes that were traditionally masculine in nature. These distinctions between a developing young gay male and other males very possibly created tension in family relationships especially with the father. According to Silverstein (1981), it may be that over time the disaffection of the developing gay male for the sex roles modeled by his father became more evident, creating an emotional distance in the father-son relationship.

This assertion by Silverstein contradicts the basic notions presented in modeling theory about how sex and gender roles are acquired by children by duplicating and incorporating such behaviors and attitudes modeled by their same-sex parent. However, Silverstein asserts that the mothers of gay males do not play a prominent role in how homosexual boys learn sex and gender roles, behaviors and attitudes. He suggests that mothers serve the function in this regard of supporting the sensitivities of their gay sons and providing an understanding of their son's natures that is not available from their fathers. Thereby gay boys may learn that it is easier to and more comfortable to relate to a female than to a male holding a traditional sex-role orientation. Following this path in sex and gender role development, gay males may become more accepting of and open to incorporating elements of femininity into their sex-role orientations that allow for greater flexibility and expressions of androgyny. This supposition does not imply, however, that the origins of homosexuality lie in disturbed father-son or mother-son relationships as proposed in traditional psychoanalytic and object-relations theory (Silverstein, 1981).

Research appears to validate the notion that most fathers behave in similar ways regardless of sexual orientation. This is perhaps because male socialization experiences are comparable for both groups of men. Society stereotypes gay men as being effeminate and less masculine in appearance and behavior. Although it has not been documented by research, it is highly possible that gay fathers remained in their closets for many years because of their sensitivity to the negativity associated with cultural images of gay men and homosexuality. The heavy pressures placed on homosexuals in our society by heterosexist and homophobic attitudes are oppressive but perhaps especially so for those gay fathers who became involved in heterosexual marriages. Many found it impossible to openly accept their true homosexual orientation and confronting their true orientation was something that was studiously avoided at all costs for many years. It is likely that the majority of gay fathers developed behavioral repertoires that were well-rehearsed culturally approved traits of masculinity, based on socialization experiences as children shared with heterosexual males. This allowed them to become involved in heterosexual marriages and adopt a traditional masculine heterosexual lifestyle. These traits and behavioral repertoires do not disappear when a man emerges from the closet to disclose his homosexuality. Public acknowledgment of homosexuality does not automatically cloak one in the cultural stereotype of effeminacy. Because it is likely that gay and heterosexual fathers closely resemble each other in degree of culturally-defined traits of masculinity, few differences can be found in the overall fathering behaviors and styles of the two groups of men (Bigner & Jacobsen, 1989a, b). When differences are noted, as those described earlier, it is possible that these can be explained by the ability of gay fathers to adopt androgynous parenting traits perhaps more readily than heterosexual fathers. In other words, gay fathers may be less threatened by incorporating and exhibiting such androgynous behaviors in their fathering relationship and role with children than heterosexual fathers.

RAISING OUR SONS:
GAY FATHERS AS MODELS OF ANDROGYNY

The changes that occur upon assuming fatherhood are numerous for most men. This developmental milestone of adulthood tends to mute the tone of traditional male gender role traits as men become required to include more behaviors that are nurturant in nature (Labouvie-Vief, 1990). This is part of the general developmental trend in gender roles observed in both men and women over the life span. Generally, for both genders, there is a tendency to converge and blend the traits of both as age increases in adulthood (Blanchard-Fields & Suhrer-Roussel, 1992). The apparent end point for both men and women is the development of a more complex pattern of gender role behaviors by middle and late adulthood. This seems to enable better coping skills as well as a wider range of flexibility in problem-solving among those with fluid rather than traditional gender role patterns (Labouvie-Vief, Hakim-Larson, & Hobart, 1987).

Psychologists have identified androgyny as the ideal gender role for men and women because of the advantages this offers individuals for healthy developmental progress (Bem, 1975). When an individual possesses traits characteristic of both genders, there is a strong gender identity of femaleness as well as maleness regardless of their biological sex. Besides that mentioned above, there are many advantages for having such a gender role orientation. Androgens are liked better than those having a traditional masculine or feminine orientation (Major et al., 1981). Adult male androgens are described as having highly developed egos, showing greater flexibility in considering options to problems, and having greater respect for individual differences in others (Costos, 1986). Androgens can be described as having an accepting attitude regarding sex, sexual relationships, and interpersonal relationships (Rosenweig & Daley, 1989). Those individuals who are rated as either masculine or androgynous are reported to have higher self-esteem than those rated as feminine or undifferentiated in their gender role (Lau, 1989).

Gender roles and identity, or the set of norms regarding the behavior and attitudes of what is masculine and what is feminine, are believed to be acquired primarily through socialization experiences over the life span. The first concepts of maleness and femaleness are initially formed at about age three as children use sex-typing as a means for gender role and identity training (Cahill, 1983; Kohlberg, 1966). External cues often assist children to learn to differentiate between what is appropriate to one sex or the other based on information about clothing, hair styles, or choice of toys and play activities (Lawson, 1989). Parental influence plays an important part in this process of how children acquire gender role and identity information. As part of the socialization process, for example, fathers participate in play activities with children that are sex-appropriate, i.e., promoting doll-play with daughters and rough-housing with sons (Jacklin et al., 1984). Cultural sources also play a role in this process. Children are bombarded with sex-appropriate behavioral cues via the media. This eventually culminates in adolescence with the peer-pressure for conformity to gender role and identity standards based largely on stereotypes (Biernat, 1991). The gender role and identity notions formed in childhood and adolescence then become modified in adulthood as many people shape these notions into ones that are more androgynous than traditional in nature.

Only a few studies have been conducted on the children of gay fathers as compared with numerous ones published on those of lesbian mothers (Bailey et al., 1995; Bozett, 1980, 1981a, b, 1987, 1988; Harris & Turner, 1986; Miller, 1979a; Paul, 1986). The majority of these have not directly observed children as subjects but data were gathered from interviews with gay fathers about their children (Gottman, 1989). Although none has focused exclusively on examining gender role or identity development of children of gay fathers, it is possible to discern the influence of gay fathers in this regard. For example, the gay fathers studied by Harris and Turner (1986) were reported to promote traditional gender role development by encouraging children to play with sex-typed toys. However, in studying the parenting styles and attitudes of gay fathers versus that of non-gay fathers, Bigner and Jacobsen (1989a, b) found data suggesting that androgynous gender role orientation was more likely among gay fathers than non-gay fathers.

Public misconception about gay men holds that they are unacceptable role models for children based on their stereotypical lack of definitive traditional masculinity in gender role behavior and identity. This myth defines gay men as being psychologically as well as physically weaker than heterosexual men. The very nature of gay men's attraction to other men is believed to be directly antagonistic to the role that social and physical power plays in the traditional notion of masculinity (Pronger, 1990). Embedded throughout such concepts are heterosexist beliefs that exist to support the necessity of the traditional gender role and identity in order for a male to be "truly" masculine. From this standpoint, only those certified as masculine (i.e., heterosexual) men are qualified to be instructors and role models of masculinity for their sons or other boys. Within this line of reasoning lies another misconception about how sexual orientation stems from gender role and identity formation: Masculine heterosexual men model masculinity appropriately for male children thus preventing them from developing into homosexuals. They promote their heterosexual orientation by teaching them the mythology of heterosexism. The flaw of such reasoning is immediately evident when it is observed that most homosexual males are the product of heterosexually oriented parents. If sexual orientation could be transmitted intergenerationally from parent to child, there should be no homosexual children produced by heterosexual parents. Obviously, this is not the case, and researchers remain unsure about the process by which sexual orientation is formed (Money, 1986; Patterson, 1995; Strickland, 1995). It is becoming increasingly evident, however, that genetics interacting with the influence of the prenatal maternal hormone environment on brain development plays a larger role than previously thought (Meyer-Bahlburg et al., 1995; Berenbaum & Snyder, 1995).

While biological factors are appearing to play a more prominent role in influencing sex-role orientation, the concept of masculinity remains to be culture-relative.

Several sources provide more evidence that sexual orientation of an adult parent has little influence on that of children (Bailey et al., 1995; Bozett, 1989a, b; Miller, 1979). In these studies, gay or bisexual fathers report that the sexual orientation of their male offspring is overwhelmingly heterosexual reflecting the rate which is thought to occur in the general population, i.e., about 90 percent are heterosexual. These studies strongly suggest that the environmental influence provided by a gay father by virtue of his sexual orientation in influencing that of his children is nil.

If gay fathers are just as likely as heterosexual fathers to have children that are heterosexual in orientation, this leaves little room for eliminating gay fathers as gender role models for their sons. But perhaps having a gay father goes one step further if we separate sexual orientation from gender role development.

The distinction that gay fathers may offer their sons is the modeling of androgyny as a gender role. The research strongly suggests that gay fathers possess such traits enabling their ability to nurture children in ways that demonstrate such diversified behavior by someone who is an adult male. Most heterosexual fathers are thought to increasingly include such feminine aspects into their roles and to do so without endangering their masculinity. It is possible that gay fathers do so with even greater ease and manifest these dualistic components in their parenting behavior more readily than heterosexual fathers (Ross, 1983). In line with this reasoning, it is possible that sons of gay fathers may be more likely than those of heterosexual fathers to adopt androgyny or incorporate more androgynous sex-role traits as they grow and mature. It is possible that gay fathers are freed to expand their interpretations of what it means to be a father far beyond the traditional meanings of fatherhood (Moreland & Schwebel, 1981). As such, this freedom to explore may allow gay fathers greater opportunities to incorporate the nurturant, expressive functions and behaviors traditionally assigned to mothers into their fathering role. Heterosexual fathers, because of their greater tendency to identify with traditional masculine sex-role orientation (Biller, 1993), may differ from gay fathers in the manner by which gender-role ideation influences their parenting behaviors and styles, despite the tendency to incorporate some feminine aspects into their behavior upon assuming fatherhood.

The benefits to children of gay fathers who adopt androgyny may become more evident as they reach adulthood and are able to participate in relationships based on equality rather than social and physical power. Research suggests that couples in which one or both partners are androgens enjoy higher levels of satisfaction with their relationship (Zammichieli et al., 1988). In such relationships, couples have been found to divide decision-making equally and deemphasize the use of power by either partner in the relationship (Cooper et al., 1985). This leads to greater relationship success than that observed in traditional couples. Furthermore, an androgynous sex role orientation is predictive of greater long-term life satisfaction that extends into the years of late adulthood than that found among those having other more traditional or undifferentiated orientations (Dean-Church & Gilroy, 1993). This gives greater credibility to the consistent findings of researchers that children experience no harmful influence to their developmental progress by being raised or living with a homosexual parent.

TEACHING SONS ABOUT HOMOPHOBIA AND HETEROSEXISM

Since it is likely that a son of a gay father will have a heterosexual orientation, gay fathers have a unique position in influencing the attitudes that their sons can adopt about masculinity and how this is to be interpreted behaviorally as well. Traditional masculine gender role and identity bases much of its power and superiority to homosexuality on the strong interest in reproduction and patriarchy. Homophobia and heterosexism are weapons of sexism that serve to maintain the traditional system of male dominance in society and notions of masculinity (Pharr, 1988; Weinberg, 1972). These notions are pervasive throughout our culture and have insidious effects upon everyone. Gay males are not immune from learning and being exposed to these oppressive attitudes. These may lie at the foundation of internalized homophobia that may motivate a substantial number of gay men to enter heterosexual marriages in which children are produced.

Androgens have been found to be more accepting of others, of their own sexuality and that of others, and to hold less tradition-bound attitudes about masculinity and femininity (Garcia, 1982; Walfish & Myerson, 1980). In this regard, gay fathers, in being more androgynous as well as having a homosexual orientation, are less likely than heterosexual fathers to hold these prejudicial notions and pass these as part of the envelope of what it means to be masculine. This is even more apparent when a gay father has disclosed his orientation and lifestyle to his children. Researchers find that rather than producing disruptive effects, disclosure promotes healthy effects for the relationship between gay fathers and their children (Bozett, 1987a, b; Dunne, 1987; Miller, 1979). Gay fathers who have disclosed their orientation in contrast with those who have not are found to have relatively stable lifestyles that often involve a domestic, committed relationship with another man. These fathers tend to spend greater amounts of time with their children, which can be adequately described as "quality" time. They are described by researchers as dependable sources of caregiving for their children and are seen by children as being authentic and genuine human beings. Nondisclosure can have unhealthy effects for both fathers and children involving issues of trustworthiness, secrecy, and lack of respect and authenticity for the father.

Disclosure to children, however, is a problematic issue for many gay fathers. Uppermost as a feared result of coming out is the potential loss of children's love (Bigner & Bozett, 1989; Bozett, 1980, 1984; Dunne, 1987). While disclosure has significant ramifications regarding the spousal relationship of gay fathers, usually resulting in separation and divorce, many report that severing their legal tie to their former wives is less disturbing than the potential loss of their parent-child relationship. Rather than producing alienation and estrangement of children, disclosure appears to promote a father-child relationship that is reported to be emotionally close and based on greater honesty and openness between father and child (Barret & Robinson, 1990; Bozett, 1980, 1985, 1987a, b; Miller, 1986; Patterson, 1992). Disclosure to children also assists gay fathers in their development of their unique personal identity as gay fathers (Bigner & Bozett, 1989; Bozett, 1980, 1981a, b). Children can be expected to neither repudiate nor disown their father following disclosure but continue to express love for him as before disclosure. Although not all children approve and enthusiastically welcome the knowledge of their father's homosexual orientation, they tend to be more accepting following disclosure than most gay fathers anticipated. The experience of disclosure and having the opportunity to see their father live a healthy, self-accepting lifestyle that models androgyny to children may serve to promote their adoption of these attitudes as well.

A commonly held belief by the legal system and other components of society is that children of gay fathers will experience serious emotional trauma by being embarrassed and stigmatized by peers should their father's sexual orientation become public knowledge. There is some truth to this notion in that children having a gay father can certainly anticipate having experiences that confront them with the effects of bigotry, prejudice, discrimination, and homophobia. Such experiences can be turned by gay fathers into valuable lessons for children to learn about the positive and not-so-positive aspects of human nature and how to deal with other's irrationality. In this regard, gay fathers can be mindful of the examples set by minority parents and those who have divergent religious or political views as they teach children how to cope with negativity because of such differences from others. Children are not known to be irreparably harmed by growing up in homes with such parents who differ from the social norms in such ways. Having a parenting experience by a homosexual parent can be strengthening for children in their character development as they learn the importance of tolerance and understanding the necessity of respecting individual differences in others (Bigner & Bozett, 1989; Rivera, 1987).

CONCLUSION

Gay fathers are in many respects no different from heterosexual fathers in their abilities to parent children effectively. However, the unique nature of gay fathers places them at the cutting edge of efforts to reinvent notions of gender roles and identity. Based on research that is scientifically sound, we know that gay fathers are highly committed to parenting responsibilities and do not harm the welfare and developmental progress of their children. Essentially, they stimulate us to broaden our thinking about what it means to be a homosexual man who also happens to be a father and how best to understand the diverse context of parenting children in alternative families.

Gay fathers need not be denied their parental rights based solely on sexual orientation issues that relate to their influence on the lives of their sons. There should be little concern about their ability to help their sons learn what it means to be a male in our society since they can be expected to portray an improved model of masculinity to children: an androgynous male. The benefits and advantages to their sons can last a lifetime and serve as a means for improving their ability to overcome the bounds of a traditional male sex role that may not be functional in contemporary society today and in their son's future.

REFERENCES

Bailey, J. M., Bobrow, D., Wolfe, M., & Mikach, S. (1995). Sexual orientation of adult sons of gay fathers. *Developmental Psychology, 31*, 124-129.

Barret, B. L., & Robinson, B. E. (1990). *Gay fathers.* Lexington, MA: D. C. Heath.

Bell, A. P., & Weinberg, M. S. (1978). *Homosexualities: A study of diversity among men and women.* New York: Simon & Schuster.

Bem, S. L. (1975). Sex role adaptability: One consequence of psychological androgyny. *Journal of Personality & Social Psychology, 31*, 634-643.

Benkov, L. (1994). *Reinventing the family: The emerging story of lesbian and gay parents.* New York: Crown Publishers.

Benokraitis, N. V. (1996). *Marriages and families: Changes, choices, and constraints* (2nd ed.). Upper Saddle River, NJ: Prentice Hall.

Berenbaum, S. A., & Synder, E. (1995). Early hormonal influences on childhood sex-typed activity and playmate preference: Implications for the development of sexual orientation. *Developmental Psychology, 31*, 31-42.

Biernat, M. (1991). Gender stereotypes and the relationship between masculinity and femininity: A developmental analysis. *Journal of Personality & Social Psychology, 61*, 351-365.

Bigner, J. J. (1972). Parent education in popular literature: 1950 to 1970. *Family Coordinator, 21*, 313-319.

Bigner, J. J. (1996). Working with gay fathers: Developmental, post-divorce parenting, and therapeutic issues. In R-J. Green & J. E. Laird (Eds.), *Lesbian and gay couple and family relationships: Therapeutic perspectives.* San Francisco: Jossey-Bass.

Bigner, J. J., & Bozett, F. W. (1989). Parenting by gay fathers. *Marriage & Family Review, 14*, 155-176.

Bigner, J. J., & Jacobsen, R. B. (1989a). Parenting behaviors of homosexual and heterosexual fathers. *Journal of Homosexuality, 18*, 173-186.

Bigner, J. J., & Jacobsen, R. B. (1989b). The value of children to gay and heterosexual fathers. *Journal of Homosexuality, 18*, 163-172.

Bigner, J. J., & Jacobsen, R. B. (1992). Adult responses to child behavior and attitudes toward fathering: Gay and nongay fathers. *Journal of Homosexuality, 23*, 99-112.

Biller, H. B. (1993). *Fathers and families: Paternal factors in child development.* Westport, CT: Auburn House.

Blanchard-Fields, F., & Suhrer-Roussel, L. (1992). Adaptive coping and social cognitive development of women. In E. E. Guice (Ed.), *Women and aging: Now and the future?* Westport, CT: Greenwood Press.

Bozett, F. W. (1980). How and why gay fathers disclose their homosexuality to their children. *Family Relations, 29*, 173-179.

Bozett, F. W. (1981a). Gay fathers: Evolution of the gay father identity. *American Journal of Orthopsychiatry, 51*, 552-559.

Bozett, F. W. (1981b). Gay fathers: Identity conflict resolution through integrative sanctioning. *Alternative Lifestyles, 4*, 90-107.

Bozett, F. W. (1984). Parenting concerns of gay fathers. *Topics in Clinical Nursing, 6*, 60-71.

Bozett, F. W. (1985). Gay men as fathers. In S. Hanson & F. W. Bozett (Eds.), *Dimensions of fatherhood* (pp. 327-335). Beverly Hills, CA: Sage.

Bozett, F. W. (1987a). Gay fathers. In F. W. Bozett (Ed.), *Gay and lesbian parents.* New York: Praeger.

Bozett, F. W. (1987b). Children of gay fathers. In F. W. Bozett (Ed.), *Gay and lesbian parents* (pp. 39-57). New York: Praeger.

Bozett, F. W. (1988). Social control of identity by children of gay fathers. *Western Journal of Nursing Research, 10*, 550-565.

Bozett, F. W. (1989). Gay fathers: A review of the literature. *Journal of Homosexuality, 18*, 137-162.

Bozett, F. W., & Sussman, M. B. (1989). Homosexuality and family relations: Views and research issues. In F. W. Bozett & M. B. Sussman (Eds.), *Homosexuality and family relations.* New York: Harrington Park Press.

Cahill, S. E. (1983). Reexamining the acquisition of sex roles: A social interactionist approach. *Sex Roles, 9,* 1-15.

Cooper, K., Chassin, L., & Zeiss, A. (1985). The relation of sex-role self-concept and sex-role attitudes to the marital satisfaction and personal adjustment of dual-worker couples with preschool children. *Sex Roles, 12,* 227-241.

Costos, D. (1986). Sex-role identity in young adults: Its parental antecedents and relation to ego development. *Journal of Personality & Social Psychology, 50,* 602-611.

Dean-Church, L., & Gilroy, F. D. (1993). Relations of sex-role orientation to life satisfaction in a healthy elderly sample. *Journal of Social Behavior & Personality, 8,* 133-140.

Dunne, E. J. (1987). Helping gay fathers come out to their children. *Journal of Homosexuality, 14,* 213-222.

Flaks, D. K., Ficher, I., Masterpasqua, F., & Joseph, G. (1995). Lesbians choosing motherhood: A comparative study of lesbian and heterosexual parents and their children. *Developmental Psychology, 31,* 105-114.

Garcia, L. T. (1982). Sex role orientation and stereotypes about male-female sexuality. *Sex Roles, 8,* 863-876.

Gottman, J. S. (1989). Children of gay and lesbian parents. *Marriage & Family Review, 14,* 177-196.

Harris, M. D., & Turner, P. H. (1986). Gay and lesbian parents. *Journal of Homosexuality, 12,* 101-113.

Hays, D. H., & Samuels, A. (1989). Heterosexual women's perceptions of their marriages to bisexual or homosexual men. *Journal of Homosexuality, 18,* 81-100.

Jacklin, C. N., Dipietro, J. A., & Maccoby, E. E. (1984). Sex-typing behavior and sex-typing pressure in child/parent interaction. *Archives of Sexual Behavior, 13,* 413-425.

Kohlberg, L. (1966). A cognitive-developmental analysis of children's sex-role concepts and attitudes. In E. E. Maccoby (Ed.), *The development of sex differences* (pp. 53-85). Stanford, CA: Stanford University Press.

Labouvie-Vief, G. (1990). Modes of knowledge and the organization of development. In M. L. Commons, C. Armon, L. Kohlberg, S. A. Richards, T. A. Gropzer, & J. Sannott (Eds.), *Adult development models and methods in the study of adolescents and their thought.* New York: Praeger.

Labouvie-Vief, G., Hakim-Larson, J., & Hobart, C. J. (1987). Age, ego level, and the life-span development of coping and defense processes. *Psychology & Aging, 2,* 286-293.

Lau, S. (1989). Sex role orientation and domains of self-esteem. *Sex Roles, 21,* 415-422.

Levinson, D. (1986). A conception of adult development. *American Psychologist, 41,* 3-13.

Levy, G. D. (1989). Developmental and individual differences in preschoolers' recognition memories: The influence of gender schematization and verbal labeling of
information. *Sex Roles, 21*, 305-324.

Maddox, B. (1982). Homosexual parents. *Psychology Today, 56*, 62-69.

Major, B., Carnevale, P. J. D., & Deaux, K. (1981). A different perspective on
androgyny: Evaluations of masculine and feminine personality characteristics.
Journal of Personality & Social Psychology, 41, 988-1001.

Meyer-Bahlburg, H. F. L., Ehrdardt, A. A., Rosen, L. R., Gruen, R. S., Veridiano, N.
P., Vann, F. H., & Neuwalder, H. F. (1995). Prenatal estrogens and the development of homosexual orientation. *Developmental Psychology, 31*, 12-21.

Miller, B. (1979a). Gay fathers and their children. *Family Coordinator, 28*, 544-552.

Miller, B. (1979b). Unpromised paternity: The lifestyles of gay fathers. In M. P.
Levine (Ed.), *Gay men.* New York: Harper & Row.

Miller, B. (1986). Identity resocialization in moral careers of gay husbands and
fathers. In A. Davis (Ed.), *Papers in honor of Gordon Hirabayashi* (pp. 197-216).
Edmonton, Canada: University of Alberta Press.

Money, J. (1986). Homosexual genesis, outcome studies, and a nature/nurture para-
digm shift. *American Journal of Social Psychiatry, 6*, 95-98.

Moreland, J., & Schwebel, A. I. (1981). A gender role transcendent perspective on
fathering. *Counseling Psychology, 9*, 45-53.

Patterson, C. J. (1992). Children of lesbian and gay parents. *Child Development, 63*,
1025-1042.

Patterson, C. J. (1994). Children of the lesbian baby boom: Behavioral adjustment,
self-concepts, and sex-role identity. In B. Greene & G. Herek (Eds.), *Contemporary perspectives on lesbian and gay psychology: Theory, research, and application* (pp. 156-175). Beverly Hills, CA: Sage.

Patterson, C. J. (1995). Families of the lesbian baby boom: Parents' division of labor
and children's adjustment. *Developmental Psychology, 31*, 115-123.

Paul, J. P. (1986). *Growing up with a gay, lesbian, or bisexual parent: An exploratory
study of experiences and perceptions.* Ann Arbor, MI: Dissertation Information
Service.

Pharr, S. (1988). *Homophobia: A weapon of sexism.* Little Rock, AK: Chardon Press.

Pronger, B. (1990). *The arena of masculinity: Sports, homosexuality, and the meaning of sex.* New York: St. Martin's Press.

Rivera, R. R. (1987). Legal issues in gay and lesbian parenting. In F. W. Bozett (Ed.),
Gay and lesbian parenting (pp. 199-227). New York: Praeger.

Rosenzweig, J. M., & Daley, D. M. (1989). Dyadic adjustment/sexual satisfaction in
women and men as a function of psychological sex role self-perception. *Journal
of Sex & Marital Therapy, 15*, 42-56.

Silverstein, C. (1981). *Man to man: Gay couples in America.* New York: William
Morrow and Company.

Strickland, B. R. (1995). Research on sexual orientation and human development: A
commentary. *Developmental Psychology, 31*, 137-140.

Turner, P. H., Scadden, L., & Harris, M. B. (1990). Parenting in gay and lesbian
families. *Journal of Lesbian & Gay Psychotherapy, 1*, 55-66.

Walfish, S., & Myerson, M. (1980). Sex role identity and attitudes toward sexuality. *Archives of Sexual Behavior, 9*, 199-203.

Weinberg, G. (1972). *Society and the healthy homosexual.* New York: St. Martin's Press.

Weinberg, M. S., & Williams, C. J. (1974). *Male homosexuals: Their problems and adaptations.* New York: Oxford University Press.

Zammichieli, M. E., Gilroy, F. D., & Sherman, M. F. (1988). Relation between sex-role orientation and marital satisfaction. *Personality and Social Psychology Bulletin, 14*, 747-754.

Familism and the Adoption Option
for Gay and Lesbian Parents

T. Richard Sullivan
Albert Baques

SUMMARY. This essay explores issues in adoption crucial for the well-being of children raised in gay and lesbian families. How gays and lesbians form families, and the legal, emotional and political implications of family formation are included. Since adoption is the choice for many gays and lesbians, a broad look at the legal and political context is necessary as well as an examination of the changing practices in adoption. The authors advocate for adoption being available to prospective adoptive parents no matter what their sexual orientation and advocate for open adoption practices based on honesty and the absence of secrecy surrounding past adoption practices. *[Article copies available for a fee from The Haworth Document Delivery Service: 1-800-342-9678. E-mail address: getinfo@haworthpressinc.com <Website: http://www.haworthpressinc.com>]*

KEYWORDS. Adoption, gay and lesbian parents, sexual orientation

GAY AND LESBIAN FAMILIES

Lesbians and gay men have always been part of family life. They are and have been sons and daughters, brothers and sisters, mothers

T. Richard Sullivan, PhD, is affiliated with the School of Social Work, University of British Columbia, Vancouver, B.C., Canada. Albert Baques, MSW, is a social worker with the B.C. Ministry for Children and Families and can be reached at #310-1225 Harwood Street, Vancouver, B.C., Canada.

[Haworth co-indexing entry note]: "Familism and the Adoption Option for Gay and Lesbian Parents." Sullivan, T. Richard, and Albert Baques. Co-published simultaneously in *Journal of Gay & Lesbian Social Services* (Harrington Park Press, an imprint of The Haworth Press, Inc.) Vol. 10, No. 1, 1999, pp. 79-94; and: *Queer Families, Common Agendas: Gay People, Lesbians, and Family Values* (ed: T. Richard Sullivan) Harrington Park Press, an imprint of The Haworth Press, Inc., 1999, pp. 79-94. Single or multiple copies of this article are available for a fee from The Haworth Document Delivery Service [1-800-342-9678, 9:00 a.m. - 5:00 p.m. (EST). E-mail address: getinfo@haworthpressinc.com].

and fathers. Lesbians and gay men have also contributed to children's lives as teachers, social workers, child care workers, family lawyers, pediatricians and in a host of other roles supportive of children. The difference today is that they seek to play these roles without deceit or pretense.

The assumption that a gay and lesbian orientation is anathema to child rearing (Benkov, 1994) reflects homophobia and the idealization of a particular family structure that is assumed to be morally superior.

In North America, the nuclear family is clearly privileged and is given special status and protection. Benkov (1994) quotes George Bush in his 1992 campaign for re-election: " . . . children should have the benefit of being born into a family with a mother and a father" (p. 112). The President emphasized that the number of parents and their gender is what matters. However, gays and lesbians challenge this narrow view of family which in the 90s accounts for a minority of North American families.

Weston (1991) explains that gay kinship ideologies challenge the belief that procreation alone constitutes kinship and that "non-biological" ties must be patterned after a biological model (as in the case of traditional adoption) or forfeit any claim to kinship status: "For many in this society, biology is a defining feature of kinship: They believe that blood ties make certain people kin, regardless of whether those individuals display the love and enduring solidarity expected to characterize familial relations" (p. 34).

Gays and lesbians embrace a much broader definition of family. Defining characteristics emphasize the quality of relationships: love, caring and understanding. Emotional and relational aspects are emphasized as opposed to the structural shape of the family. Gay and lesbian families include more than blood relatives: "They are increasingly defined as intimate groups of people who love and support one another" (Pollack, 1995, p. 18).

The major shift in gay and lesbian family creation today is not only the increasing number of gays and lesbians choosing parenthood, but that gays and lesbians are having children after coming out. Lesbian mothers and gay fathers are no longer so afraid of going public. Moreover, there is an increasing number of gay and lesbian parenting organizations that provide networking, support and visibility.

Changes in the contemporary social climate more favorable to the recognition of diverse families are partly due to the contribution of the gay rights movement. Heterosexual procreation is clearly only one of many forms of family creation. Changing patterns in divorce, adoption, and reproductive technology all have implications for whether children will be raised by their biological parents (Benkov, 1994; Eichler, 1988). Artificial insemination, adoption, surrogacy and joint parenting arrangements are only a few of the ways gays and lesbians are choosing to become parents. In many cases, they meet with broader social acceptance today, but in addition to the emotional, financial, and legal considerations that face any parent, lesbian and gay parents must also contend with societal homophobia and the absence of legal equality (Pollack, 1995).

THE LEGAL CONTEXT OF HOMOPHOBIA AND HETEROSUPREMACIST FAMILISM

In Canada, most legislation pertaining to marriage, families and the welfare of children is framed at the provincial level. In 1994 the provincial government of Ontario introduced a bill to eliminate discrimination against lesbian and gay relationships and families (Bill 167). The attempt to introduce this legislation and its ultimate defeat represented a very significant moment in the history of the struggle of gay men and lesbians to achieve full human rights. Bill 167 announced one of the strongest anti-discrimination initiatives in North America.

On May 19, 1994, Bill 167 barely passed its first reading. The campaign for Equal Families represented a very intensive and well publicized lobbying that gained attention and respect on an international scale. However, it did not overcome the prejudice and political cynicism which was legitimized by Premier Rae's "free vote," a departure from party discipline on the floor of the legislature that enabled members to follow their own inclinations rather than party policy. On June 9, 1994, the bill was defeated. Its defeat enraged the gay and lesbian community and thousands of men and women, disappointed and angered, marched in the streets of Toronto (Ursel, 1995).

Despite the fact that similar legislation passed in British Columbia with very little debate three years later, the vitriolic debate over same-sex spousal benefits in Ontario served to show how different our world is from that of other parents and how vulnerable our families are within an unstable political climate. For Bernstein and Stephenson

(1995) it underscores "how thin is the blanket of security we have attempted to weave around our family" (p. 3).

In Canada and the U.S., there is little to protect lesbian and gay parents and their children from subjective and arbitrary decisions. For decades the courts reflected society's opinion that lesbian and gay parents were unfit without any scientific research to support these assumptions (Pollack, 1995). Lesbians and gay men were seen as aberrants, immoral, selfish, undesirable, disturbed, diseased, molesters and perpetrators of abuse. Children needed to be protected from gays and lesbians. It was believed that children should not be exposed to lesbian and gay relationships. Gays and lesbians lost custody disputes or had visitation restrictions imposed. Gays and lesbians were forbidden to foster or adopt a child and were declared publicly inferior. Florida has statutorily prohibited lesbians and gay men from adopting since 1977. New Hampshire's ban on gay foster care and adoption became effective in 1987. The Nebraska Department of Social Services last year implemented a state-wide ban on foster parenting by lesbians and gay men (Gooch, 1996).

Since homophobia is so pervasive in our culture, writes Benkov (1995), "advocates must be able to respond to beliefs that lesbian and gay parents, simply by virtue of their homosexuality, harm their kids" (p. 58). The artefacts of homophobia include: the beliefs that the children will themselves become gay; children will suffer psychological damage as a result of stigmatization; children will suffer from family disruption assuming that gay relationships are more transient; and finally, that children will be sexually molested by their gay parents.

Research does not confirm any of these fears. No differences in well-being and normative functioning have been found between children reared by heterosexuals and those raised by lesbian or gay parents (Patterson, 1992). "The fear that children raised by homosexuals will grow up to be lesbian or gay suggests that it would be awful if that were the case. In order to prove that they are worthy parents, lesbians and gay men have had to prove that they are not likely to raise children who will grow up to be like them" (Benkov, p. 62). This despite the fact that studies of over 300 offspring of gay or lesbian parents in twelve different samples have indicated no evidence of significant disturbances in the development of sexual identity (Patterson, 1992).

Benkov (1994) stated that "those who argued that children should be protected from stigmatization by being separated from their lesbian or gay parents essentially shift the burden of responsibility from society onto parents–onto the victims rather than the perpetrators of bigotry" (p. 64). Rather than attempt to completely shield children from prejudice, Benkov proposes that responsible adults should make efforts to help them deal with it. Benkov advocates that children should be helped to deal constructively with discrimination so that they might develop significant strengths such as independent thinking and self-assertion in respect of their convictions. Research on other minority children and the role of their families and communities in contributing to resilience and effective coping has relevance for the children of gay and lesbian parents. Gloria Johnson Powell's (1983) extensive review of research on the factors associated with effective coping among Afro-American children concludes that family and community play a critical role in mediating the potentially adverse effects of prejudice. Similarly, Norton (1983) studied the family life patterns by which black children develop a critical perspective on prejudice which offsets its negative effects. Comparisons that do not begin with presumptions of inferiority and superiority among diverse family forms can be more instructive than invidious.

With respect to some of the other negative stereotypes attached to sexual minority families, Golombok and her colleagues (1983) found that transience has not been any more characteristic of lesbian relationships than of women's heterosexual relationships, and study after study has shown that perpetrators of sexual abuse are disproportionately heterosexual men (Benkov, 1994). In one of the most critical and comprehensive reviews of the research on children in gay and lesbian households, Charlotte Patterson (1992) concluded:

Overall, then, results of research to date suggest that children of lesbian and gay parents have normal relationships with peers and that their relationships with adults of both sexes are also satisfactory. In fact, the findings suggest that children in custody of lesbian mothers have more frequent contact with their fathers than do children in custody of divorced heterosexual mothers. There is no evidence to suggest that children of lesbian or gay parents are at greater risk of sexual abuse than other children. (p. 1034)

However, lesbian and gay parents do not have the same protection as our heterosexual counterparts. Though gays and lesbians in relationships see each other as family, lesbians and gays are denied the legal benefits of marriage. Our bonds are invisible and not recognized. When children are involved and couples split up or the legal parent dies, children's relationships with their non-biological or non-adoptive parents are still in jeopardy in most jurisdictions. In a society where social benefits are conditioned by compliance with unitary forms of marriage and family, the legal benefits of marriage are structured to favor those forms. Inequity is the inevitable consequence in areas basic to family well-being, including health insurance, tax and inheritance law, housing and employment.

Those in the gay and lesbian community who are critical of efforts to gain legal recognition of spousal partnerships are to be commended for their pride in asserting an alternative to patriarchal traditions, but they miss the practical considerations of access to social benefits that many lesbian and gay parents cannot afford to miss. Recent changes to the Canadian Human Rights Act offer more explicit protection against some forms of discrimination, and legislative changes in British Columbia enable lesbian and gay parents to adopt and treat their obligations to the children reared in their households with equality before the law both prior to and after dissolution of the domestic partnership. Nonetheless, both Canada and the United States fall short of recognizing gay and lesbian spousal unions to the extent of affording them status equal to marriage. As in the days when sectarian agencies proscribed the adoption placement of children in mixed marriages (meaning either inter-racial or inter-denominational), a message is communicated concerning the social valuation of those families.

ADOPTION REVISITED

Adoption is defined by the Child Welfare League of America as a legal and social process that gives full family membership to children not born to the adoptive parent(s) (Child Welfare League of America, 1978). It is a variably complicated legal process replete with inherent dilemmas and conflicting interests. References to the "adoption triangle" acknowledge a dynamic lifelong process involving three primary parties: the birth parents, the child and the adoptive parents. Each member of the triad is affected by different personal, psychological, social and legal factors (Cosgrove & Silzer, 1991). Whether all corners are acknowledged at any one time, members of the adoption triangle are bound together for life (Axness, 1995).

The literature on adoption notes that in an era of change the institution of adoption has altered dramatically. Some of the critical contextual changes of the era have included changes in sexual mores, the civil rights movement, changes in the institution of marriage, the increasing divorce rate, reproductive technology and consumerism (Cole & Donley, 1990). The declining number of babies available for adoption[1] is a consequence of some of these social changes. On the other hand, the increasing number of special needs children[2] requiring stability and permanence has been a growing concern in the last decade.

The most serious challenge, as stated by Sachdev (1984), has come with adoption workers' recognition of the need for a significant shift in value orientation and adoption policy, and the need to mediate and balance the conflicting rights and interests of the principal members of the triad. Adoption is no longer a quiet arrangement between adoptive applicants and adoption workers, in which almost invisible unmarried mothers and totally invisible biological fathers remained in the background. It is now a more complex and fluid social institution (Lipman, 1984).

Until the 1970s, adoption practices showed vestiges of ancient societies in that they were designed to meet the need primarily of middle and upper class infertile couples for children. Twentieth century adoption policy and practice in the western world has emphasized similarities rather than differences between adoptive and biological families: Closed records and secrecy were required for this purpose (Whiteford, 1988). A characteristic of North American culture is the strong value placed on the traditional nuclear biological family. This perspective has construed all other families, including adoptive families, as substitute at best and deviant and deficient at worst (Hartman & Laird, 1990). Until very recently, adoption policy and practice were shaped largely by this value and the consequent effort to model adoption as much as possible on biological parenting. Therefore, traditional adoption attempted to equal the genetic birth experience. There was no distinction between adopted children and children born to a family, on the presumption that adoptive parents would inevitably regard their children as their own and the birth parents would forget the pain and go on with their lives (Hartman & Laird, 1990). However, the emerging view holds that adoption is a unique, life-long experience not to be confused with genetic parenting (Cole & Donley, 1990, p. 280).

The changes taking place in this field have had a significant impact on the members of the adoption triangle. Moreover, professionals of different disciplines–adoption agency personnel, the legal profession and mental health practitioners, have had to refocus their approach following these changes. The degree of complexity in adoption is often a source of confusion in professionals' attempts to understand a complex family process which demands an interdisciplinary approach (Brodzinsky & Schechter, 1990).

Parents who cannot keep their infants and have no supports for the resolution of their losses may harbour longstanding emotional conflicts. Sorosky, Baran and Pannor (1978) reported that for most birth mothers, the relinquishment and adoptive placement was a traumatic experience that remained with them throughout their life. According to Baran and Pannor (1990), most of the psychological problems that affect every member of the triad are directly related to the secrecy and anonymity of the closed, traditional system of adoption. These authors are convinced that the closed system must be replaced with a new philosophy and practice of adoption. This new practice should be based on openness and honesty wherein adoptions transpire within a policy framework that recognizes the interests of all concerned parties (Baran & Pannor, 1990). Open adoption allows communication between birth parents and adoptive parents. Baran and Pannor (1990) defined open adoption as "the process in which the birth parents relinquish legal rights to the adoptive parents. Both sets of parents retain the rights to continue contact and access to knowledge on behalf of the child" (p. 318).

Deymick and Seymour (1988) identified four levels of open adoption: restricted open adoption, in which arrangements are made for pictures and information about the child's development to be sent to the birth parents (through the agency) for a specified time following placement; semi-open adoption, in which birth parents meet the people who will be adopting the child but no identifying information is shared; full open adoption, in which both sets of parents meet and identify information; and continuing open adoption, in which birth parents and adoptive parents establish a plan for continuing contact with one another and the child over the course of the child's development. According to Silber and Martinez (1985), open adoption offers benefits for all the members of the triad. For the adoptee, open adoption can provide answers to questions asked without the shame or guilt associated with secrecy. Moreover, when there is open communication within the family, the adoptee does not have to feel that s/he is being disloyal to his/her adoptive parents by being curious about the birth parents. For birth parents, open adoption allows them to better process their feelings of grief. They may feel they have made a plan for their child instead of feeling that they have abandoned the child to an unknown and uncertain future. Adoptive parents generally report that upon meeting the birth parents, they no longer fear them. Through open adoption, the birth parents give the adoptive parents permission to be parents and bonding with the child is facilitated as a result of this permission (Silber & Martinez, 1989).

According to Baran and Pannor (1990) the benefit of open adoption to the child is probably the most significant. Since adoptees live with a dual identity, the adoptive family exists in the child's real world, while the birth parents are in the fantasy world. Adoptees may feel that there is something wrong or bad with them to have been rejected by their birth parents. Adopted persons may need contact with both families; "the adoptee who is able to see, touch, and feel the birth parent can believe the fact that the person does care, but could not, at the time of the child's birth, take care of him or her" (p. 331).

Rappaport (1983) referred to open adoption as "normalized" adoption. Rappaport pointed out a critical contradiction in traditional adoption practice: "in an open and democratic society like ours, open and aboveboard procedures should be the norm, and closed, secretive operations should be the exception" (p. 174). The concept of normalization gives open adoption the character of a healthier and more positive experience and process than traditional adoption. For Silber and Martinez (1989), traditional or closed adoption should not be viewed as acceptable practice.

The practice of open adoption is steadily growing, particularly in the United States and Canada. However, open adoptive placement has been the exception, not the norm, and practice wisdom will need to evolve to guide changing practice. As professionals become more comfortable with open adoption, they will be in a better position to aid adoptive parents to accept open placements and end anonymity and secrecy as they steer a new course through this complex relationship.

The converging trends toward open adoption and equality of treatment of gay and lesbian parents before the law may present additional challenges to practice.

WHO CAN ADOPT?

In most Canadian jurisdictions, only singles and legally married couples may adopt. This too is changing rapidly. In British Columbia, a new Adoption Act was proclaimed in 1996. Under the new Act, all adults over the age of 19 may apply to adopt. In keeping with the Canadian Charter of Rights and Freedoms, barriers which discriminate against common-law couples and same-sex couples are removed. However, in all cases the courts will only grant an adoption order when it is in the best interest of the child.

The new Act also challenges the secrecy around adoption. After the bill became law, the provincial government launched a year-long campaign to advise birth parents and adoptees that their records may be opened unless they register a disclosure veto or a no-contact declaration with the Ministry for Children and Families. The birth records of an estimated 50,000 children are to be made accessible to birth parents unless they file a veto.

The new Act also regulates private and international adoptions. Thorough assessments of prospective parents will be mandatory before children can be placed either through the Ministry or a licensed adoption agency and only the Ministry and non-profit adoption agencies are authorized to handle adoptions. International adoptions must be conducted in the best interests of the child in keeping with the terms of the Hague Convention on the Protection of Children.

The new Act allows for an ongoing exchange of information between the adoptive parents and the birth parents. This extends to people who did not have this option under the former Act dating from 1957. Birth fathers who want to be involved in planning for their children can make their interest known through a birth father's registry. Birth mothers will have 30 days, as opposed to 10, to consent to adopt, even though the child has been placed for adoption and they may arrange with adoptive parents for an open relationship.

The British Columbia Adoption Act extended a recognition of diverse family forms earlier reflected by New York State legislation, which as of 1995 formally recognized the right of unmarried couples–

gay or straight–to adopt children. For gay and lesbian parents and prospective parents changing the social construction of marriage and family and the institutions that uphold those constructions is more than an abstract theoretical exercise. It is an imperative. Assuring an optimal social experience for their children compels it. Such is the intergenerational covenant. If social scientists and experts in human development agree that lifting the veil of secrecy and denial is better for the developing adoptee, then so too we must agree that opening the closet door to acknowledge the diversity of ways parents come to that role is better for our children. Minority families can provide a buffer and a meta-perspective that better equips their children for the risks they will encounter in a world where prejudice may assault their persona and their prospects. But effective anticipatory socialization rests on self-knowledge and self-identification as part of a recognized social group. From this perspective, the secrecy of the closet can be no less laden than denying the existence of birth parents. By extension, if gays and lesbians are not permitted to form families by adoption, then what is communicated to gay and lesbian families formed in other ways? If we are not fit to adopt, then what does that communicate to our natural and step-children? The implicit threat of discriminatory policy has loomed long over custody cases involving gay and lesbian parents. In the face of government assurance that recent Human Rights decisions are not intended to go so far as to legalize gay marriages or extend marital and family benefits to these households, gay and lesbian activists insist that we will accept nothing less. When we do so insist, we are upholding a covenant to protect our children. It is the same covenant that reaches for a small hand in a crosswalk, that insists on driver's education, marches against child labour and for clean air, and that seeks not to burden our children's future with our debt and disastrous social policy. Is that not a pro-family agenda?

THE PROMISE AND THE PRACTICE

In preparing this paper, one of the authors interviewed two sets of parents who had recently completed the adoptions of their infant children. One of the mothers was herself a social worker with prior professional experience in adoptions and a former colleague of the author's. The author met the other parents when he was asked to complete a home study as part of the requirements for the completion of an adoption they had initiated in the United States. When their adoption was finalized six months later, the author asked to interview them about their experience. Their observations were elicited in open-ended response to two broad questions: How would you describe your contacts with the agencies through which the adoption of your child was achieved? And how would you describe your transition to parenthood? Their responses reflect some of the realities facing lesbian and gay prospective parents during this period of transition. Not surprisingly, this small sample related some experiences unique to lesbian and gay parents and many others common to all parents.

Pollack (1995) writes that as more gays decide to experience parenthood, it becomes more obvious that they have the same motives as those of straight people: "the simple desire to raise a child and build a family" (p. 33). Within the lesbian community, those motives have been subjected to self-conscious critical examination. Grounded in her experience as a lesbian, an adoptee, a mother and a social worker, Linda, one of the informants to the development of this paper, reflected on the larger context of racism, classism and economic exploitation wherein patriarchal dominance has traditionally been reproduced and sustained through the structure of family relations. That analysis brings a vigilance to the emulation of heterosexual family formation in the lesbian community. In that vein, Vaughn (1987) writes: "we are overlooking something, that there are issues we should be seriously addressing. . . . I am concerned about what we, as lesbian mothers, unconsciously pass on to our children. All of us have grown up as the unwilling participants in a system that has negated our very existence. Unless we shake ourselves free of dominant cultural values and assumptions about The Family we are almost bound to recreate something which not only doesn't work, but which oppresses us" (p. 24).

Although Linda's view comes from a more global perspective, other informants related a perspective grounded in the daily routine of raising a child in need of a family. They too reflected on their encounters with homophobia during their transition to parenthood. Dylan was only few weeks old when one of the authors met him. In his role as a social worker, one of the authors helped Dylan's parents, Ricardo and Allan, complete the post-placement visits leading to the legal finalization of his adoption. Allan applied to an adoption agency in Philadelphia and by reciprocal agreement between jurisdictions, a home study was completed in Vancouver by a social worker employed by the Ministry of Social Services. This home study was initially done for the purpose of Allan and Ricardo adopting an older child. Both Allan and Ricardo had been interviewed in the home study, though Allan was the single applicant since a same-sex common law couple could still not adopt in British Columbia. Allan sent their home study off to Philadelphia. He explained that the agency in Philadelphia "could not find families fast enough for the children. They had more children than they could find homes for." The agency was happy to accept their application, and in about two weeks, a phone call informed them that Dylan had been born. Allan flew to Philadelphia and met four-day-old Dylan. Allan recalled:

> My biggest problem was dealing with Canadian immigration. Because all of this happened so fast and you are dealing with bureaucracy, of course, most of the paperwork had not been processed although I had sent everything off. I had to deal with getting Dylan back into Canada. I thought Canada being such a humane place, they would be on my side, but no, they were not in the least interested in accommodating me. In fact, the Consulate in New York City told me that I could not bring Dylan back into Canada. When I asked: "What should I do with him?," bearing in mind that Dylan was four days old, she said I must place him in foster care. Then when I asked: "How do I do that? I don't know anybody in Philadelphia," she replied curtly: "Well, you are not bringing him into Canada." I implored her to consider: "How would you feel about having to leave your child in a strange country and not have the child return home with you?"

The legal process dealt a lighter hand than her dismissive response: "He is not your child." Allan continues:

> I had not slept, had never been in Philadelphia. The whole thing was very stressful. Dylan was there waiting for me . . . eventually, I shared custody with the agency. I was dealing with a newborn baby, all on my own, in a strange city, in another country, trying to deal with things like diapers and formula and having nobody in the city to turn to. I was in Philadelphia for a week and immigration still had made no progress. When I got Dylan's

passport, we went back to Canada with the fear that he would not be allowed into the country.

A few months later, the post-placement visits were completed and the finalization of the adoption was recommended. Allan and Ricardo were asked to express what was positive about their relationship, what their strengths were. Most of the time, since same-sex couples cannot adopt legally as a couple, they cannot be open about being gay or lesbians, so they are unable to share what may be one of their major strengths, their relationship. In this situation, Allan was the petitioner but his marital status read: "single but involved in a committed, long term, common-law relationship with a person of the same sex." Ricardo and Allan were surprised when Allan was asked if he wanted Ricardo on Dylan's birth certificate. The Family Court of Philadelphia recognized Dylan's adoptive parents, Allan and Ricardo, as both being legal guardians. That birth certificate and the recognition it conveys marked a rare and meaningful benchmark by which this couple marked their transition to parenthood. Allan and Ricardo stated that the way they differ most from other families is how they are perceived, but fundamentally, they think they are exactly the same. Ricardo added: "We are going to encounter problems with people who may not like the fact that Dylan has been raised by two men, but at the moment we have received lots of support."

They are trying to build a network of friends and other adoptive parents or same-sex couples with children. They are aware of the need for other couples to share guidance, advice and common experiences, but reported an increasing amount of confidence in themselves as parents. Their philosophy is to try to instill in Dylan a sense of pride in who he is. Ricardo and Allan believe that people accept you if you are very comfortable and accepting of yourself: "The more comfortable and accepting we are of our family, the more comfortable and accepting people are of us."

Homophobia is encountered in all aspects of our lives. It seems that social policy will yield as often to partisan ignorance as to emerging social knowledge, and myth may exert more influence than conclusions drawn on fact. It is for this reason that gay and lesbian parents and the helping professions mandated to serve children must together constitute themselves a community committed to correct unjustified misconceptions that could otherwise burden a child's progress. Parents' sexual orientation in itself is irrelevant to children's well-being. Gays and lesbians are creating families and as Benkov states: "when lesbian and gay men create families, these families are part of the world and influence it as much as they are influenced by it" (p. 13). The closet demands passivity, but parenting requires proactivity in the interests of our children. As parents and as social workers we are obliged to lift the yoke of yesterday's prejudice from the tomorrows of our children.

NOTES

1. Cosgrove and Silzer (1991) explain in their *Review of Adoption Services in British Columbia* the impact of societal changes over adoption; "since World War II," they explained, "when a young woman had a child out of wedlock, she most often relinquished her baby because she had few supports and single motherhood was not socially tolerated . . . In the early 1970s things changed. The supply of healthy adoptable infants declined for a number of reasons: increased use of birth control, increased availability of abortion, and greater social acceptance and financial support of single mothers . . . In addition, the individual rights movement has affected the adoption scene. Adoptees are claiming the right to know their birth and adoption histories. Birth fathers are claiming their parental rights over children relinquished for adoption" (p. 3).

2. Special needs children are considered those who are ten years and older; have serious physical, intellectual, or emotional problems; are from minority groups; or are members of large sibling groups. The consideration of these children as adoptable goes hand in hand with the concept of permanency planning, which refers to efforts to maintain a child's birth family whenever possible, to return a child to his birth family as soon as possible and, failing either, to establish for the child legally nurturant relationships with caring adults preferably through adoption. These children are usually permanent wards of the State/Province, and their surrender for adoption was usually involuntary. Due to the different connotations of the adoption of special needs children, this paper focuses on infants surrendered voluntarily.

REFERENCES

Axness, M. W. (1995). "Authentic Beginnings, Real Bonds." NASW California News. December/January 1995. p 11.

Baran, A. & Pannor, R. (1990). Open Adoption. In Brodzinsky, D. & Schechter, M. (1990). *The Psychology of Adoption.* New York: Oxford University Press.

Benkov, L. (1994). *Reinventing the Family. Lesbian and Gay Parents.* New York: Crown Trade Paperbacks.

Bernstein, J. & Stephenson, L. (1995). Dykes, Donors & Dry Ice: Alternative Insemination. In Arnup, K. (ed.) *Lesbian Parenting. Living with Pride and Prejudice.* Charlottetown, Canada: Gynergy Books.

Brodzinsky, D.M. & Schechter, M. (ed.) (1990). *The Psychology of Adoption.* New York: Oxford University Press.

Child Welfare League of America (1978). *Standards of Adoption Service*. New York: CWLA.

Cole, E. & Donley, K. (1990). History, Values, and Placement Policy Issues in Adoption. In Brodzinsky, D. & Schechter, M. (1990). *The Psychology of Adoption*. New York: Oxford University Press.

Cosgrove, J., & Silzer, N. (1991). *A Review of Adoption Services in British Columbia*. Report prepared for the Ministry of Social Services and Housing. B.C.: Unpublished.

Demick, J. & Seymour, W. (1988). Open and Closed Adoption: A Developmental Conceptualization. *Family Process, 27*, 229-249.

Eichler, M. (1988). *Families in Canada Today*. Toronto: Gage Educational Publishing Company.

Golombok, S., Spencer, A., & Rutter, M. (1983). "Children in Lesbian and Gay Single-Parent Households: Psychosocial and Psychiatric Appraisal." *Journal of Child Psychology and Psychiatry, 24*, 551-572.

Gooch, B. (1996). My Two Dads. *Out*. February 1996 issue.

Hartman A., & Laird, J. (1990). Family Treatment After Adoption. In Brodzinsky, D. M. & Schechter, M. (ed.). *The Psychology of Adoption*. New York: Oxford University Press.

Lipman, M. (1984). Adoption in Canada: Two Decades in Review. In Sachdev, P. *Adoption: Current Issues and Trends*. Toronto: Butterworths (pp. 31-42).

Norton, D. G. (1983). "Black Family Life Patterns, the Development of Self and Cognitive Development of Black Children." In Powell, Gloria J. (Ed.) *The Psychological Development of Minority Children*. New York: Bruner Mazel Publishers.

Patterson, C. J. (1992). "Children of Lesbian and Gay Parents." *Child Development*. Vol. 63 (pp. 1025-1042).

Pollack, J.S. (1995). *Lesbian and Gay Families. Redefining Parenting in America*. New York: Franklin Watts. The Changing Family.

Powell, G. J. (Ed.) (1983). *The Psychological Development of Minority Children*. New York: Bruner Mazel Publishers.

Rappaport, B. (1983). *The Open Adoption Book: A Guide to Adoption Without Tears*. New York: Macmillan.

Sachdev, P. (1984). *Adoption: Current Issues and Trends*. Toronto: Butterworths.

Silber, K., & Martinez Dorner, P. (1989). *Children of Open Adoption*. Texas: Corona Publ.

Sorosky, A. D., Baran, A., & Pannor, R. (1978). *The Adoption Triangle*. New York: Anchor Press.

Ursel, S. (1995). Bill 167 and Full Human Rights. In Arnup, K. (ed.) *Lesbian Parenting. Living with Pride and Prejudice*. Charlottetown, Canada: Gynergy Books.

Vaughn, J. (1987). A Question of Survival. In Pollack, S. & Vaughn, J. (ed.) *Politics of the Heart. A Lesbian Parenting Anthology*.

Weston, K. (1991). *Families We Choose. Lesbians, Gays, Kinship*. New York: Columbia University Press.

Whiteford, H. (1988). *Special Needs Adoption: Perspectives on Policy and Practice*. Major Paper. University of British Columbia, School of Social Work.

It's All a Matter of Attitude: Creating and Maintaining Receptive Services for Sexual Minority Families

Linda Poverny

SUMMARY. Should programs and services for sexual minority families be mainstreamed in organizations which traditionally cater to a predominantly non-gay, non-lesbian clientele, or should these services and programs remain the purview of specialized organizations catering to the needs of gay and lesbian clientele?

This essay begins with a discussion of the unique needs of sexual minority families and the current rationale for separate versus integrated services, including an examination of the pressures on these families and what they need to sustain family life. Arguments for and against separate and integrated services are explored.

Second, the ways an organization's culture shapes receptivity and responsiveness to a particular client population are considered. Attitudes, values, beliefs, and symbols dictate an agency's norms and prescribe its organizational behavior. Ultimately this is reflected in the programs and services to parents and children.

Finally, this essay sets out an argument for developing a continuum of service delivery strategies for promoting family life among sexual minorities. *[Article copies available for a fee from The Haworth Document Delivery Service: 1-800-342-9678. E-mail address: getinfo@haworthpressinc.com <Website: http://www.haworthpressinc.com>]*

KEYWORDS. Sexual minorities, families, community services, specialization versus mainstreaming

Linda Poverny, PhD, is Professor, School of Social Work, University of Southern California.

[Haworth co-indexing entry note]: "It's All a Matter of Attitude: Creating and Maintaining Receptive Services for Sexual Minority Families." Poverny, Linda. Co-published simultaneously in *Journal of Gay & Lesbian Social Services* (Harrington Park Press, an imprint of The Haworth Press, Inc.) Vol. 10, No. 1, 1999, pp. 95-113; and: *Queer Families, Common Agendas: Gay People, Lesbians, and Family Values* (ed: T. Richard Sullivan) Harrington Park Press, an imprint of The Haworth Press, Inc., 1999, pp. 95-113. Single or multiple copies of this article are available for a fee from The Haworth Document Delivery Service [1-800-342-9678, 9:00 a.m. - 5:00 p.m. (EST). E-mail address: getinfo@haworthpressinc.com].

Any discussion about agencies providing services to sexual minority families must start with a clear understanding of what is meant by "family." Historical definitions of family are exclusively a heterosexual phenomenon, based on laws that are predicated on religious values and beliefs. Access to marriage, the presumed prerequisite to creating a family, is monopolized by the state, thus imposing a barrier to those unable to obtain legal recognition of their relationships (Ingram, 1996; Weitzman, 1975). More contemporary definitions of family include single parent families, blended families and unmarried partners with children, as long as they are heterosexual. This article expands the definition of family, building on the work of Poverny and Finch (1988), Patterson (1994), and Pollack (1995) among others, who redefine family more inclusively basing their definitions on characteristics such as continuity of commitment by members over time, mutual obligation, and economic and domestic interdependence (California Commission on Personal Privacy, 1982).

IDENTIFICATION OF NEED

Using the above definition, creating and maintaining programs and services for gay and lesbian families becomes feasible, as the target population can be elaborated. These families consist of same sex couples with or without children, or perhaps sexual minority single parents (Slater, 1995). Children may be adopted, or from a prior heterosexual union, or as a result of artificial insemination. Some of these families may be raising grandchildren, or have responsibility for a partner's elderly parent(s). These families do not appear on the surface to be any different from their heterosexual counterparts. As Patterson (1994) and others repeatedly point out, lesbians and gay men have struggled with legal, economic, religious and social discrimination against their family relationships. This has been particularly true when it comes to their children, yet despite the hardships, gay men and lesbians continue to form families.

Sexual minority identification creates unique obstacles, pressures and experiences, which burden these families by imposing an unequal social status and negative societal valuation. As with racial and ethnic minorities, sexual minority families experience social isolation, marginalization, discrimination, and a refusal on the part of the majority culture to grant basic civil rights (Benkov, 1994; Gibson, 1977; Pollack, 1995). These rights, such as equal access to medical insurance coverage for partners and their children, access to family and bereavement leave, and adoption laws that equally favor heterosexual and homosexual couples, have yet to become widespread, institutionalized policies and practices in our social service agencies, or in our workplaces (McNaught, 1993). Dominant cultural norms reinforcing a heterosexual bias creep into the fabric of our social programs through the organizational behavior exhibited by professionals and others.

Without a keen awareness on the part of mainstream service organization board members, administrators and staff, about how pervasive and insidious these biases are, agencies reputed to support family life become instead, agents of continuing conflict, contradiction, and inequity. In many major metropolitan areas this is the primary reason why gay and lesbian communities create parallel social service delivery systems. Separate services are perceived to be a more effective means of supporting and nurturing sexual minority families. This option, however, is not always feasible for every community.

THE MAINSTREAM SERVICE SECTOR

Assessing the responsiveness of community mental health services to San Francisco's gay, lesbian and bisexual clientele was the focus of a study by Rabin, Keffe and Burton (1981), in which important insights about non-sexual minority workers in a mainstream organization were revealed. First, staff tended to evaluate "need" based on how many clients from a certain group were utilizing services. Since it appeared that few sexual minorities used the agency, staff reported that specialized programs were unwarranted. The author's observation on this finding is noteworthy:

> . . . many sexual minority clients did not seek services because they find programs inappropriate or hostile, or because staff are unfamiliar with or negative about gay male, lesbian, and bisexual lifestyles. (p. 295)

Second, the study results point out that professionals tend to avoid discussions of sexuality in general, while still viewing sexual orientation as an issue of sex thus suggesting serious discomfort with issues relevant to sexual minority status. Third, many staff viewed homosexuality from a pathological viewpoint when assessing a client's psychological healthfulness. These respondents expressed negative attitudes toward both sexual minority clients and colleagues. Finally, participants in the study were reluctant to embrace a recommendation to appoint an organizational liaison to the lesbian and gay community who would assist with intakes, referrals and act as a consultant to the heterosexual staff.

These types of negative attitudes and behaviors exhibited by traditional organizational members lead to two basic questions addressed in this article: Should programs and services for sexual minority families be mainstreamed in organizations which traditionally cater to a predominately non-gay/non-lesbian clientele, or should these services and programs remain the purview of specialized organizations, catering predominately to the needs of sexual minority clients? A corollary concern is: What would be the necessary organizational conditions under which one can plan and implement appropriate, responsive and effective services for sexual minority families within a traditional public/private organizational framework? This becomes particularly relevant when community size and resources limit the amount of available support for a separate social service network.

In order to explore these questions, a brief overview of the types of concerns and issues with which sexual minority families struggle establishes the need for developing sensitively thought out services. This discussion is limited to typical problems faced by members of these families, and is not meant to cover specific additional stresses and stigmas accompanying socioeconomic class, ethnicity or race. The focus here is on concerns germane to gay and lesbian parents and children in general, and what is required to sustain and foster family life, both for those living in large cities as well as smaller communities.

In the second section we look at the rationale, and pros and cons for alternative versus mainstream agencies offering such services. In this discussion, how and in what ways an organization's culture shapes and prescribes the degree to which services can be receptive and responsive illustrates how sensitivity is a matter of attitude when creating and maintaining services for sexual minority families. Organizational theories such as those of Schein (1985) and Ott (1989) suggest values, beliefs and symbols dictate an agency's norms and expectations, as well as provide prescriptions for organizational behavior. These factors are then reflected in services and programs created for parents and children. Attributes of the agency's culture either suggest inclusiveness or exclusivity. In the face of intolerance, an argument can be made for developing a continuum of service strategies, whenever possible. Suggestions are provided for creating and maintaining receptive organizational milieus.

The last section offers recommendations for establishing reciprocal relationships between mainstream and specialized service organizations in an effort to foster a dynamic interplay among programs and practitioners resulting in expanded attitudes and behaviors, values and beliefs. Forming a functional community of truly "family friendly" organizations among both types of service delivery systems is recommended as optimal when addressing the needs of minority community members, as neither is sufficient on its own.

REALITIES OF FAMILY LIFE

Depending upon where you live your experience as a gay or lesbian parent, or as the child of such parents may differ. The sociocultural conditions extant in a small town or mid-size city tend to push sexual minority families underground, creating a high degree of isolation, concomitant with a diminished sense of social connection (Harry, 1988; Miller, 1989). This phenomenon of reduced social involvement tends to occur with both the heterosexual and the homosexual "community," albeit for different reasons. A narrowly conceived idea about family and traditional cultural norms generally predominates in these communities, creating a cultural ethos that marginalizes, stigmatizes and fears sexual minorities–(homophobia). The development of any specialized organizations or services supporting family life is unlikely in this context because many of these families remain hidden, or "in the closet." This invisibility makes it difficult to establish a critical mass able to support alternative social services (Harry, 1988).

The resulting realities for sexual minority families in small to mid-size towns are often: (1) a lack of access to appropriate services, (2) judgmental, negative attitudes from service providers toward family members, (3) policy and decision makers that are unaware of the need for sensitive programs and services, and (4) a lack of understanding regarding the unique concerns and problems faced by these families, along with inadequate knowledge of intervention strategies, and available resources. Even in large metropolitan cities, to a somewhat lesser degree, similar cultural conditions prevail.

Obsolete yet powerfully negative values, behaviors and fears influence the social attitudes of community members who often become institutional managers, staff and volunteers in our family and child welfare organizations (Mallon, 1992). Unlike smaller communities, large metropolitan areas have an identified, varied and complex set of institutional arrangements working as a countervailing force–namely the lesbian and gay community. This social construct provides involvement opportunities and a sense of connectedness for families. The family is defined broadly, with multiple norms, values and attitudes expressed about family life. In most major metropolitan areas today a plethora of tailored services and programs, as well as providers of specialized services are meeting many of the family needs of sexual minority members (Pollack, 1995).

Frightfully little research explores lesbian/gay family concerns and problems, resulting in sparse reporting on family life. Yet the work that currently exists identifies and reports on typical psychosocial problems faced by all families (Bozett & Sussman, 1990; Ricketts & Achtenberg, 1987), and involves the various types of organizations set up to address these issues (Greeley, 1994; Harry, 1988; Mallon, 1992; Patterson, 1994; Sullivan, 1994). To illustrate the point, think about the myriad social service institutions generally mobilized to address issues such as adoption, foster parenting, infertility and family planning, child custody, family counseling, child guidance, child welfare, juvenile justice and family violence. How culturally competent and receptive are these organizations and delivery systems when it comes to appropriately meeting the needs of sexual minority families? Most likely, the reasons for which services are sought are similar to heterosexual families, but the additional circumstance of sexual minority status creates complexities that require considered attention.

Living with Fear

In order for social service organizations to become competent service providers they must be willing and able to pinpoint and understand the unique conditions facing these families, along with their palpable effects. Sexual minority individuals live with a constant, and sometimes pervasive threat from many sectors in their environment. Fear may surround employment, or the lack of equal employment opportunities and benefits (Poverny & Finch, 1985). Bigotry and alienation pose a threat to every facet of life, as does losing one's standing in the community. These underlying tensions might be brushed aside by an individual who is single, but for parents, there is no escape from the immediate constraints felt from the legal establishment over such issues as visitation, child custody, or parental status. Additional sources of fear come from perceived or experienced harassment, or from feeling ostracized. Whether real or imagined, these worries and fears about neighbors, schools, religious and social institutions become potential sources of strain, rather than sources of support, a unique artifact of being a sexual minority parent (Slater, 1995). Research conducted by Ross (1983) supports this contention that it may not be the *actual* social reaction from the outside that is critical to how one feels, but rather it is what one *perceives* the societal reaction to be.

Alternatively, the children of gay and lesbian families are not immune to the fear of reprisal. Bozett (1988) studied 19 children of gay fathers and found that some of these children engaged in activities that managed the image outsiders had of their households. In an effort to avoid harassment by children of heterosexual parents, these children refused to have other children to their homes, and they would fail to refer to their father's partner. In addition, Bozett (1987) identified a unique stressor facing parents, as they adapted to their parental role within a subculture that is largely single and childless. Conflicting demands between parental obligations, and social and community obligation can be more taxing for sexual minority families than for heterosexual based families. Overall, there is little, if any, research to assist gay men and lesbians on the psychosocial transitions from being single, or in a coupled relationship, to adoptive, foster, or biological parenthood.

Furthermore, the regulations governing adoption and foster care make it exceedingly difficult for lesbians or gay men to embrace these roles and responsibilities (Rickett, 1991). In most states, only one member of a sexual minority couple is regarded as the legal parent, effectively relegating the other parent to an unequal status (Polikoff, 1990). Many questions arise for prospective parents as Patterson (1994) illustrates in an article on same sex couples considering parenthood. But where can these families go to discuss their concerns and questions? Where can informed answers be found? The general consensus among authors on sexual minority families is that the alternative social service sector is still the delivery system of choice.

Sullivan's (1994) work on foster placement of sexual minority youth is illustrative. In large cities gay/lesbian foster homes for sexual minority adolescents have proliferated over the last several years to address the serious needs of these youth. Services have been handled almost exclusively by private, specialized, voluntary agencies. Observing that many of these children fail in traditional placement, due to a lack of understanding about their unique needs and circumstances, Sullivan points out how "gay and lesbian communities are undertapped resources for potential family foster homes" (p. 298). Why, if these youth do markedly better in sexual minority families, are traditional child welfare organizations reluctant to mine these rich resources? The ethical imperative among helping professionals, and among Social Workers in particular, would suggest attending responsibly and respectfully to the complexities brought to bear by these youth, however, the attitudes and values expressed by agency policies and practices continue to hinder appropriate and sensitive placements (Mallon, 1992; Schneider, 1991; Sullivan, 1994).

In order to sustain and promote family life, same sex parents and their children want to be able to interact with organizations and institutions that are free of prejudicial attitudes, discriminatory practices and heterosexist bias. Much of the prejudice and discrimination comes from inadequate and biased laws. Furthermore, one only need look at a child's birth certificate to see how public policy is value laden. The names of a male and a female parent are specifically requested at birth. This institutional bias potentially affects the child for a lifetime. The inability of same sex couples to gain legal standing through "marriage" illustrates another disadvantage affecting children and parents alike. Faulty assumptions about gay and lesbian parents and their children continue to perpetuate the development and reinforcement of negative social policies governing family life (Healy, 1996; Huber, 1996). Yet mainstream agency personnel have done little to counteract these insensitivities toward sexual minority families. In California, for instance, as recently as 1995-96, Governor Pete Wilson reversed a state policy allowing gay adoptions and lobbied strenuously to ban same sex marriages. There was no visible opposition from the child welfare community, or in the professional media.

SEPARATE BUT NOT EQUAL TO MAINSTREAM SERVICES

A review of the literature on family programs and services with which sexual minorities need to interact points to several widespread problems with mainstream organizations. The most glaring systemic obstacles creating unresponsiveness are enumerated as follows:

1. Agency goals do not always fit with the realities and circumstances of sexual minority family life. For example, promoting single parent adoptions to the exclusion of same sex couple adoptions undermines the reality of established and strong sexual minority unions.
2. Agency policies and practice generally have a heterosexist bias, evidenced by such tangible indicators as intake forms requesting information on "father" and "mother," to less obvious indicators such as behaviors that express negative attitudes toward sexual minority persons. Sexual minority status, for example, is not treated as an affirming characteristic, but rather it is considered a "problem."
3. Agencies lack current research and information on the bio-psycho-social development of sexual minority individuals and families, parenting, and other family related issues, as well as in-depth knowledge of appropriate community resources.
4. Agencies act inflexibly around coordinating and cooperating with available specialized services in sexual minority communities where they exist, and are reluctant to create linkages to these specialized agencies.

While problems certainly exist with these organizations, they also provide a breadth and depth of service that is hard, if not impossible, to replicate in a subcultural community.

Most traditional family-oriented service organizations are characterized by intricate ties to social policy mandates, relationships with power holders, and have public legitimacy and oversight. These organizations rely on predictable resources and have professional staffing, along with relative stability and geographic decentralization within their communities. These factors make this traditional public/private agency framework a force to be reckoned with, rather than circumvented or ignored. Additionally, ties to academic institutions, professional organizations and accrediting bodies make mainstream delivery systems accountable for at least minimal standards of care and services, often going beyond these minimums by experimenting with new models and practices in ways that are difficult to achieve in alternative delivery systems. Traditional service agencies belong to lobbying organizations, network among themselves and share their collective influence in their fields of expertise. Finally, traditional, mainstream organizations are available to all socioeconomic groups within society, making them the service sector of choice, for all but the most wealthy. These benefits ought to be available to lesbian and gay community members just as they are to non-sexual minority people.

The specialized service sector offers different opportunities and constraints. It is more attuned to, familiar and comfortable with the needs of the sexual minority population. Alternative services are more receptive, and also more accountable to the minority community. This suggests, however, that public oversight can be more laissez-faire and even baseline standards run the risk of being compromised. Private adoptions by sexual minority couples, for example, may use independent attorneys who are comfortable working with sexual minority members, rather than going through a traditional child welfare agency. This same couple may contract for an independent home study with a sexual minority Social Worker in private practice (Ricketts & Achtenberg, 1987). These approaches, while supportive, informed and affirming, remove the process from public and professional view and reinforce the notion that same sex couple adoptions should be a private rather than a public matter. This approach perpetuates the notion that sexual minority families should reside in that world of "don't ask, don't tell," the results of which are continuing marginalization. The final result is that mainstream family welfare organizations are not held accountable for providing appropriate essential services.

Where the alternative social service delivery system does some of its best work is in providing supportive social services, legal advocacy, and recreation and socialization opportunities to families. Organizations such as the Lyon-Martin Lesbian/Gay Parenting Services (LGPS), or the Lesbian Choosing Children Project (LCCP), or the Los Angeles Gay and Lesbian Community Service Center (GLCSC) offer programs consisting of support groups for prospective parents, childbirth education classes, information and referral services, workshops on parenting issues at different developmental stages in a child's life, and panels covering topics such as considering parenthood, legal issues, adoption, and getting pregnant, to name only a few. Providing necessary information and support, along with recreation and socializing normalizes family life. These community organizations also make it a point to reach out to professionals from mainstream agencies to promote the link and establish a relationship. Unfortunately, all too often this is not reciprocated. Herein lies the greatest challenge: how to assist mainstream organizations to become increasingly receptive and responsive to sexual minority families.

Organizational Culture Prescribes Organizational Behavior

The transmission and perpetuation of an organization's culture comes from a number of variables, most specifically from hiring selection and removal of members who do not meet the organization's expectations; socialization of organizational participants; reward systems that maintain and promote or value certain behavior, and ongoing communication both verbal and non-verbal. Mitroff and Kilmann (1984), Ott (1989) and Schein (1985) assert that one of the most powerful ways to understand the culture of an organization is to examine its taboos. Taboos are powerful because they represent the organization's sense of itself. Taboos erect a set of boundaries clarifying behavior–certain acts are permitted and others are not. All organizational members are affected by the workplace culture, and what the workplace prescribes for its members becomes transmitted to its clientele. As Martin and Siehl (1983) remarked about culture, it is an "organizational control mechanism, informally approving and prohibiting some patterns of behavior" (p. 52).

McNaught (1993) attempts to bring issues of workplace taboo and culture to the fore as he describes organizational behavior related to sexual minority issues in the typical workplace:

> . . . gay workers today will hear a gay joke, the inappropriate use of language, such as a "fag" or "dyke" comment, or an AIDS joke. They are also likely to see an anti-gay cartoon or article taped to an office file cabinet or door. And if it's not a homophobic comment, it is often a heterosexist remark or question that creates anxiety, anger, frustration, or distractions . . . it is hard work to dodge questions about what you did for Thanksgiving and what your weekend plans are. It is difficult to refrain from

participating in discussions about family and friends. It takes energy to keep from being honest about oneself. (pp. 2 & 7)

He goes on to observe that closeted gay and lesbian employees generally do not make or receive personal phone calls in front of co-workers, dread putting up a picture of their partner or family, and often do not attend office social functions unless they come alone. The taboos are clearly communicated within the organization about what is acceptable and what is not. For workers who are "out," that is, where their sexual orientation is known to various organizational members, expressions of values such as the following are often a focus of discussion:

I believe that the (organization) giving benefits to your gay partner puts your relationship at the same level as mine, and that's not right. Many of the problems we face today as a society are due to the breakdown of the family. We need to support heterosexual families. (McNaught, 1993, p. 80)

These perspectives are widespread as evidenced in an op-ed piece for a major metropolitan newspaper, in which Harris (1996) recently wrote, "(e)ven social liberals who are sympathetic to the gay civil rights movement often pause at the notion of gays raising kids" (p. B5).

With these negative values and beliefs ingrained, a shared understanding develops among agency members about sexual minority issues. These unspoken norms are transmitted and infused throughout the activities of the organization, from how sexual minority workers are treated, to how and in what ways sexual minority clients are served. These attitudes affect not only the delivery of services, but also influence what services and programs are delivered.

Although agency leadership plays an important role in transmitting and maintaining the organization's biases, they too can become trapped in, and by, the power of the organization's culture. Administrators need to lead their organizations in new directions, using policy changes that emphasize non-discrimination in programs and services, as well as in employment and benefits. In order for sexual minority family-friendly services to be successful, each worker, each leader and all other organizational members must participate in amending the collectively defined culture. This can only occur if organizational members acknowledge that issues of sexuality are, indeed, a part of the agency's ethos.

Burrell and Hearn (1989) write in *The Sexuality of Organizations* that " . . . the absence of sexuality from the vast majority of organizational analyses may be explained as part of a desexualizing of organizations . . . " (p. 12). Supporting their observation, there is a scarcity of writing in the administrative literature on human service organizations that grapples with managing sexuality as it pertains to sexual orientation. Yet, other management dilemmas related to sexuality, such as sexual harassment, have become readily discussed and researched. Both administrators of family focused organizations and professionals have a responsibility to investigate the role attitudes, values and concomitant behaviors play in their agencies. In order to alter an agency's culture toward a more inclusive stance, not only must sexuality in general be dealt with, but in particular, the subject of sexual minorities must be addressed.

Organizational theorists as well as diversity trainers tell us organizational behavior is acquired or learned (Farson, 1996; Jellison, 1993; McNaught, 1993; Schein, 1985). This means that it can be molded and shaped to reflect shifts in the culture of an organization over time. Armed with this perspective, change agents within traditional family oriented organizations can feel hopeful that their agencies can become more receptive and inclusive of sexual minority families. Although one's personal values and beliefs may differ somewhat or considerably from one's workplace culture, significant alterations can occur around how organizational personnel behave with, and on behalf of, sexual minority clients. Many devoutly Christian child welfare and family services workers, for example, who personally do not believe in abortion or divorce, work responsibly and ethically with clientele where both of these conditions or issues are present. Providing services to our clientele in a tolerant and non-judgmental way does not connote acceptance of all of their behavior. Making a distinction between tolerating difference and endorsing lifestyles, according to McNaught (1993), is a very important delineation and it will need to be reinforced over and over again if the agency is to become more inclusive and innovative.

RECOMMENDATIONS FOR CHANGE

There are two foci for change efforts: the individual and the organization. First, the culture of each organization, including its professed and latent values and beliefs, normative practices, taboos and symbols ought to be assessed using criteria related to sexual minority inclusion, receptivity and expressed need. Look at the organization's mission statement. Within its commitment to serving a particular client population, are sexual minority individuals and families included? Do the policies and practices of the agency support and encourage involvement and participation by sexual minorities, both as clients and workers? If not, what barriers exist? Looking at the organization's administrative, personnel and service mandates and practices for clues, the leadership needs to attend to necessary revisions. Policies setting forth a clear declaration that sexual minority individuals and families are to be responsibly and appropriately served, can begin the shift in culture.

If legislative mandates exclude sexual minority families from service, the agency needs to take a stand on these issues. Advocates for family planning provide a useful illustration of this point. In the United States anti-abortion activists have attempted to destroy funding and legislative support for family planning services. In the face of great controversy, these organizations have not retreated from the abortion question, and have continued to serve their clientele, while advocating on their behalf under threats of extinction. Gay men and lesbians are familiar with the social and legal obstacles facing them, so if an organization expresses a supportive, advocacy stance, sexual minority individuals and their children will be more likely to perceive that organization as approachable.

Social service workers should reassess personnel policies and benefits that may discriminate against sexual minority workers. The way in which different groups of workers are treated makes a statement to the entire organization about how, and who, is valued, desired and worthy. Over ten years ago, Hidalgo (1985) called on the National Association of Social Work (NASW) members to realize that:

> policies are guides for action, and it is time that the actions of social workers and their professional practices reflect respect, concern, and consideration for the needs of lesbians and gay men –be they clients or colleagues. (p. 129)

This challenge remains today; to assure policies supporting sexual minority workers and clients are developed, and to assure their implementation. Managers and administrators must learn to act as role models for tolerance. Professionals and support staff need consistent examples of appropriate organizational behavior. Board members and volunteers must know that expressions of homophobia, like sexism, racism, or anti-Semitism are not tolerated.

Taking Initiative to Create a Continuum of Service

Mainstream organizations need to take the initiative to advance collaborative relationships with lesbian and gay organizations in cities where an alternative service delivery network exists. Activities such as appointing liaisons from mainstream to specialized service organizations and vice versa, forming ad hoc groups around mutually defined topics, and recruiting volunteers from the gay and lesbian community, are all ways to promote an integrated continuum of service. In addition, computer technology now provides access to wonderful resources for agencies in areas where specialized services do not exist. Lesbian and gay parent chat groups, listings of sexual minority social services and family resources are readily available via the Internet.

Cyberspace allows even the smallest town to take advantage of the information and resources available throughout the world. With today's readily affordable computer hardware and servers, every social service agency and provider can access relevant information on, resources for, and communicate about issues pertaining to the sexual minority family. This is creating a sense of being a part of a larger community for those in rural hamlets and mid-size cities. Possibilities abound using this technology to augment existing organizational arrangements. By providing access to people, resources, and advocacy groups in geographic areas unable to support the suggested blending of specialized and traditional programs and providers, service integration becomes feasible electronically.

Individual Staff as the Focus of Change

As the organization begins a cultural shift, all members need specifically focused continuing education, experiences and exposure to gay and lesbian clients, staff, and the host of issues surrounding these families. No one likes to admit to being prejudiced; therefore agencies must work hard at providing venues for staff, volunteers and board members to feel safe while they explore and express truly felt attitudes, beliefs and behaviors about sexual minority families. Focusing educational and training opportunities on lesbian/gay issues in the workplace is an important place to begin. This training focus can dovetail with the cultural shifts occurring simultaneously in the organization.

Using an outside diversity training consultant can be useful to the organization, because they specialize in working in milieus where sexual minority workers usually represent a hidden minority, and they focus the training not on client or customer issues, but instead on the ways people in the room think, act and feel toward each other. Ultimately, the facilitator leaves the organization which offers participants a certain level of comfort to engage in the process. The organization should hire a well-versed trainer who has experience and expertise in working with groups around issues of homophobia and heterosexism in the workplace. Creating a dialog among staff and providing experiential exercises is challenging but can assist with personal awareness and individual behavioral growth.

As the workplace becomes more responsive and receptive to lesbian and gay employees, education on client issues can begin. Professionals from the gay and lesbian community are expert informants on issues pertaining to community resources, service needs, and problems. Where these individuals are not easily identified, the Internet may be used. Reducing fear in the minds of organizational members, by exposing myths about sexual minorities and their families, by providing corrective information based on scientific study, and by experience, is the best antidote to prejudice, negative values and inappropriate actions. Most homophobic behavior is a result of misinformation, fear and lack of exposure. Thus an organization that provides learning opportunities reinforces its desire to shift not only policies and procedures, but also assists its employees in the change process. Slow progress is to be expected, but organizational change is possible and does occur. Members need to be reminded periodically that it is in the spirit of serving their clients that these issues have relevance to their work.

Finally, professional organizations and Schools of Social Work should partner with mainstream agencies to develop curriculum modules that address sexual minority family issues. Some curriculum examples include theories of individual and family development, parenting issues during the child's life cycle, and sexual minority foster or adoptive parenting. Once again, using the Internet for "distant learning" provides a growing means by which continuing education courses can be offered to people unable to attend professional meetings, or travel to universities.

CONCLUSION

Creating and maintaining receptive services for sexual minority families requires dedicated organizational members from both mainstream organizations and the alternative service delivery sector. Since sexual minority families live in two worlds, they are more familiar with traditional organizations than most traditional organizational members are familiar with them, their subcultural community, and its resources. The burden of change is with the mainstream family-focused organization. The changes necessary in organizational culture, and in the attitudes and behaviors of workers, administrators and volunteers are not only possible, they are essential, if lesbian/gay families are to have equal access to services, and appropriately developed programs, with responsive personnel to meet their needs.

Each service sector has an expertise that needs to be exploited to its fullest advantage on behalf of the client population. There are small examples that light the way. In Los Angeles, Vista Del Mar, a mainstream adoption agency, strives to include lesbian and gay prospective parents in their orientation meetings, in their prospective parent support groups, and in the adoption process. This organization, while not perfect, does continually work on helping its staff members become more responsive and receptive to the needs of prospective sexual minority parents. Meanwhile the Los Angeles Lesbian and Gay Community Center provides the specialized knowledge and support needed as individuals or couples contemplate adoption. Thus, by establishing a continuum of services, where providers contribute their best effort, optimal service delivery is offered to the sexual minority family.

REFERENCES

Benkov, L. (1994). *Reinventing the family: The emerging story of lesbian and gay parents*. New York: Crown.
Bozett, F. W. (1987). Gay fathers. In F. W. Bozett (Ed.), *Gay and lesbian parents*, pp. 3-22. New York: Praeger Press.

Bozett, F. W. (1988). Social control of identity by children of gay fathers. *Western Journal of Nursing Research*, 10, 550-556.

Bozett, F. W., & Sussman, M. B. (1990). (Eds.) *Homosexuality and family relations.* New York: Harrington Park Press.

Burrell, G., & Hearn, S. J. (1989). The sexuality of organizations. In S. J. Hearn, D. L. Sheppard, P. Trancred-Sheriff, & G. Burrel (Eds.). *The sexuality of organization.* Beverly Hills, California: Sage Publications.

California. (1982). *Commission on personal privacy.* Supplement 1. Sacramento, California, 14-15.

Farson, R. (1996). *Management of the absurd: Paradoxes in leadership.* New York: Simon and Schuster.

Gibson, G. G. (1977). *By her own admission: A lesbian mother's fight to keep her son.* Garden City, New York: Doubleday.

Greeley, G. (1994). Service organizations for gay and lesbian youth. *Journal of Gay & Lesbian Social Services: Issues in Practice, Policy and Research, 1,* 3/4, 111-130.

Harris, S. (July 11, 1996). Just your normal life with 2 fathers. *Los Angeles Times*, p. B5.

Harry, J. (1988). Some problems of gay/lesbian families. In C. S. Chilman, E. W. Nunnally, & F. M. Cox (Eds.), *Variant family forms.* Newbury Park, California: Sage Publications.

Healy, M. (July 13, 1996). House backs curbs on gay marriages. *Los Angeles Times*, pp. A1 and A12.

Hidalgo, H. (1985). Administrative, personnel, and professional policies of social work agencies and institutions: Lesbian and gay issues. In H. Hidalgo, N. Peterson, & J. Woodman (Eds.), *Lesbian and gay issues: A resource manual for social workers.* New York: NASW Press.

Huber, S. (July 10, 1996). Public shows ambivalence about same-sex marriages. *Los Angeles Times*, pp. A1 and A15.

Ingram, C. (July 9, 1996). Wilson, Lungron back bill against gay marriages. *Los Angeles Times*, pp. A1 and A20.

Jellison, J. (1993). *Overcoming resistance: A practical guide to producing change in the workplace.* New York: Simon and Schuster.

Mallon, G. (1992). Gay and no place to go: Assessing the needs of gay and lesbian adolescents in out-of-home care settings. *Child Welfare, 71,* 6, 547-556.

Martin, J., & Siehl, C. (1983, Autumn). Organizational culture and counter culture: An uneasy symbiosis. *Organizational Dynamics,* pp. 52-64.

McNaught, B. (1993). *Gay issues in the workplace.* New York: St. Martins Press.

Miller, N. (1989). *In search of gay America.* New York: Harper and Row.

Mitroff, I. I. & Kilmann, R. H. (1984). Corporate taboos as the key to unlocking culture. In R. A. Kilmann, M. J. Saxton, R. Serpa, and Associates (Eds.), *Gaining control of the corporate culture.* San Francisco: Jossey-Bass.

Ott, S. J. (1989). Organizational culture: Concepts, definitions, and a typology. In J. S. Ott (Ed.), *The organizational cultural perspective.* Pacific Grove. California: Brooks/Cole Publishers.

Patterson, C. J. (1994). Lesbian and gay couples considering parenthood: An agenda for research, service, and advocacy. *Journal of Gay & Lesbian Social Services: Issues in Practice, Policy and Research, 1, 2,* 33-53.

Polikoff, N. (1990). This child does have two mothers: Redefining parenthood to meet the needs of children in lesbian mother and other nontraditional families. *The Georgetown Law Journal, 78,* 459-575.

Pollack, J. S. (1995). *Lesbian and gay families: Redefining parenting in America.* New York: Franklin Watts Pub.

Poverny, L. M., & Finch, W. A. (1985). Job discrimination against gay and lesbian workers. *Social Work Papers,* 19, 35-45. Los Angeles, California: University of Southern California.

Poverny, L. M. & Finch, W. A. (1988). Gay and lesbian domestic partnerships: Expanding the definition of family. *Social Casework: A Journal of Contemporary Social Work, 69, 2,* 116-121. New York: Family Service of America.

Rabin, J., Keefe, K., & Burton, M. (1981). Enhancing services for sexual minority clients: A community mental health approach. *Social Work, 31, 4,* 295-297.

Rickett, W., & Achenberg, R. (1987). The adoptive and foster gay and lesbian parent. In E. W. Bozett (Ed.), *Gay and lesbian parents.* New York: Praeger Press, pp. 89-111.

Ricketts, S. W. (1991). *Lesbian and gay men as foster parents.* Portland, Maine: National Child Welfare Resource Center for Management and Administration.

Ross, M. W. (1983). *The married homosexual man.* London: Routledge and Kegan Paul.

Schein, E. H. (1985). Content and levels of culture. In E. H. Schein (Ed.), *Organizational culture and leadership.* San Francisco: Jossey-Bass.

Schneider, M. (1991). Developing services for lesbian and gay adolescents. *Canadian Journal of Mental Health, 10,* 133-151.

Slater, S. (1995). *The lesbian family life cycle.* New York: The Free Press.

Sullivan, R. T. (1994). Obstacles to effective child welfare services with gay and lesbian youth. *Child Welfare, 73, 4,* 291-304.

Toronto Gay Fathers (1981). Gay fathers: Some of their stories, experiences, and advice. Toronto: Gay Fathers of Toronto.

Weitzman, L. T. (1975). To love, honor, and obey? Traditional legal marriage and alternative family form. *Family Coordinator, 24, 4,* 531-548.

Index

Achieved status, motherhood as an,
    27-46
Achtenberg, R., 100,104
Adoption
    Adoption Act (British Columbia,
        Canada, 1996), 56-57,88-89
    case studies of, 89-93
    community and social service
        needs, 96-99
    definitions of, 84-85
    historical perspectives of, 85-88
    legal doctrines and issues, 56-58,
        81-84
    open adoption, xvii, 79,86-89
    special needs children and, 93
    Vista Del Mar (Los Angeles),
        mainstreaming adoption
        agency, 111
Adoption Act (British Columbia,
    Canada, 1996), 56-57,88-89
AIDS diagnoses, impact on legal
    issues, 12-13
Anderson v. *Luoma* (1986), 18
Andrews, K., 18,54,57
Androgynous behavior models, xvii,
    61,67-71
Antoniuk, T., xvi, 47
Arnup, K., xvi, 1,4,5,7,13,14,58
Artificial insemination, legal doctrines
    and issues, 4,13-21,27-46,
    80-81
Ascribed status, motherhood as an, 27-46
Axness, M.W., 85

Bailey, J.M., 64,68,69
Baques, A., xvii, 79
Baran, A., 86,87
Barret, B.L., 62,64,72

Beargie, R., 5
Bell, A.P., 62
Bem, S.L., 67
Benkov, L., 64,80,81,82-83,96
Benokraitis, N.V., 64
Benson, S., 13-14
Berenbaum, S.A., 69
Bernstein, F.A., 16-17
Bernstein, J., 81-82
Bezaire v. *Bezaire* (1980), 5,8
Biernat, M., 68
Bigner, J., xvi,xvii, 61,62,63,64,
    65,66,72,73
Bill 167 (Ontario, Canada, 1994),
    4,21,81-82
Bill 31, amendment to Family
    Relations Act (British
    Columbia, Canada, 1997), 53
Bill C-33, amendment to Human Rights
    Act (Canada, 1996), 21-22
Biller, H.B., 70
Blanchard-Fields, F., 67
Blended families, 27-46
Bottoms v. *Bottoms* (1995), 3,22
Bottoms, S., 3,22
Bowers v. *Hardwick* (1986), 2
Boyd, S., 4,12,14
Bozett, F.W., 62,64,65,68,69,71,
    72,73,100,101
Brantner, P.A., 9
Brell, A.P., 62
British Columbia College of
    Physicians and Surgeons, 14
British Columbia Council of Human
    Rights, 13-14
Brodzinsky, D.M., 86
Brophy, J., 12
Burrell, G., 107
Burton, M., 97
Bush, G., 80